THE NEW MIDDLE AGES

BONNIE WHEELER, *Series Editor*

The New Middle Ages is a series dedicated to pluridisciplinary studies of medieval cultures, with particular emphasis on recuperating women's history and on feminist and gender analyses. This peer-reviewed series includes both scholarly monographs and essay collections.

PUBLISHED BY PALGRAVE:

MAINTENANCE, MEED, AND MARRIAGE IN MEDIEVAL ENGLISH LITERATURE

Kathleen E. Kennedy

MAINTENANCE, MEED, AND MARRIAGE IN MEDIEVAL ENGLISH LITERATURE

Copyright © Kathleen E. Kennedy, 2009.

First published in 2009 by
PALGRAVE MACMILLAN®
in the United States—a division of St. Martin's Press LLC,
175 Fifth Avenue, New York, NY 10010.

Where this book is distributed in the UK, Europe and the rest of the world,
this is by Palgrave Macmillan, a division of Macmillan Publishers Limited,
registered in England, company number 785998, of Houndmills,
Basingstoke, Hampshire RG21 6XS.

Palgrave Macmillan is the global academic imprint of the above companies
and has companies and representatives throughout the world.

Palgrave® and Macmillan® are registered trademarks in the United States,
the United Kingdom, Europe and other countries.

ISBN: 978–0–230–60666–1

Library of Congress Cataloging-in-Publication Data

Kennedy, Kathleen E. (Kathleen Erin)
    Maintenance, meed, and marriage in medieval English
literature / Kathleen E. Kennedy.
        p. cm.—(The new Middle Ages)
    Includes bibliographical references.
    ISBN 0–230–60666–0 (alk. paper)
    1. English literature—Middle English, 1100–1500—History and
criticism. 2. Literature and society—Great Britain—History—To 1500.
3. Master and servant in literature. 4. Marriage in literature. 5. Support
(Domestic relations)—Great Britain. 6. Master and servant—Great
Britain—History. 7. Social history—Medieval, 500–1500. I. Title.

PR275.S63K46 2009
820.9'001—dc22   2008041904

A catalogue record of the book is available from the British Library.

Design by Newgen Imaging Systems (P) Ltd., Chennai, India.

First edition: June 2009

10 9 8 7 6 5 4 3 2 1

Printed in the United States of America.

From Dr. K
To Mr. K and Mrs. K, and always JPK

CONTENTS

ACKNOWLEDGMENTS

In a project this long in the preparation, the group of people who have provided professional advice and personal support is large and no list can possibly be exhaustive. My sincere thanks to all who have helped to shape and drive this book toward completion. My dissertation committee guided these thoughts through their infancy, and the editorial staff at *Yearbook of Langland Studies* has been enormously generous with suggestions as I honed different elements of this argument. Likewise, the reader for The New Middle Ages kindly provided both positive reinforcement and productive criticism. Cordial thanks also goes to the Society of the White Hart, particularly past presidents Sharon Michalove and Douglas Biggs, who have heard many portions of this book in the form of conference papers, and who have supported me through all phases of my career.

Personally, I must thank the friends and colleagues old and new who keep me going through success and crisis. When I could crawl no further, Leigh Ann Craig and Hanne Blank carried me. Heather Corinna, Patricia Price, David Perry, and Bob Klepfer, too, helped me in more ways than they know.

I wish to offer a final thanks to one seldom recognized: Mr. Dennis Jordan, your wry joy and insistence that even rural junior high students ought to think opened doors for me. Thank you.

CHAPTER 1

INTRODUCING MEDIEVAL MAINTENANCE

When nonspecialists ask me about the topic of this book, usually I begin with an admittedly imperfect analogy: the Mob. "Imagine that you're in Chicago in the 20s or 30s," I say, "and the Mob is everywhere." I point out that the Mob may own the police or the judges in your area, leading some to receive "more" justice than others. However, your corner grocer may have connections, too, and so his store is better stocked than those in other neighborhoods. Maybe you face less street crime in your neighborhood than some because the Mob's watching your area. From your perspective, the Mob does bad things: it kills people, and it corrupts government and law. But at the same time you recognize that the Mob does good things as well: it can make obtaining goods and social services easier and less expensive, and may curtail some kinds of crime.[1] "Now imagine," I tell my listeners, "that the Mob is everywhere, and that there's not just one, but many, throughout the cities and across the countryside. That's medieval England. That's what this book is about."

Of course, the "Mob" is not really what this book is about, although I am not the first medievalist to use the allusion.[2] As far back as 1979, Barbara Hanawalt was noting that "the most highly organized associations were those of the barons and their households whose criminal activity fell between that of a white collar criminal and an early Sicilian Mafia type."[3] While Hanawalt used the Mafia analogy to exemplify the criminality of the nobility and gentry, I use it in a more culturally situated manner, referencing the way that men were deeply embedded in relational networks characteristic of various social institutions. Nevertheless, a crucial element to medieval relationships may not occur to the postmodern reader with only a vague notion of "the Mob," and that element is service. Americans tend to lack a notion of service: people may have *joined* the Mob, but in the popular imagination they did not *serve* the Mob, or their boss inside that organization.[4] To be explicit, therefore, this book explores the culture of relationships between different kinds of masters and men in late medieval England. I seek to add to our knowledge of how these relationships formed, and why, and what they meant to the participants. In particular, I have become interested in the degree to which the medieval English were not autonomous agents in the same way that modern people are. I integrate literary criticism with historiography in a way that expands our understanding of history, while at the same time giving us a more historically accurate way of reading literature. In this book, I concentrate on relationships between lords and their retinues, as well as other service-based relationships that were seen in the Middle Ages as analogous to that between lord and retainer, including that between husband and wife.

Among historians it is generally accepted that service was central to medieval English society. The most stereotypical form of noble service bound a knight to a lord through an indenture of retinue. Such bonds, and their rewards, were indicated most formally by indentures, or more temporarily by wearable status markers such as livery (uniforms), collars, or badges. The various tokens of service indicated both the lord's care for the servant and the servant's duty to the lord. Both noble and retainer benefited from the arrangement. Patronage resulting from such relationships could also take the form of special treatment in many areas of life, including real estate and the law. In fact, a recognized tie with a lord, the magnate's "good lordship" or "love," could on its own be cultural capital for those interested in acquiring local power.

While at the noble end of the social register, retainers, affines, and their lords shared a relational culture with menial servants and their masters: the relationships were different in degree, but not in kind, if you will. A master of servants, be he the senior man in a small farming household, head of a bustling mercantile business, or a lord called to Parliament, had a special relationship with his servants that was recognized as having social, religious, and legal dimensions. The *paterfamilias* took on the spiritual care of his servants, ensuring that they lived modest Christian lives. Being head of any household made him responsible for upholding his contract with his servants, providing them with the payment, food, or housing specified in the contract. Socially, a master was responsible for his servants in his community, and the law, that special, codified branch of social rules, determined that as long as he fulfilled his contract, the master had a legal standing that his servant did not. Certainly, this outline of master-servant relations is a highly generalized one, but medieval society understood this picture of service relations to be a social ideal.

Indeed, master-servant relations were used as analogies for a range of other social relations, including the relationship of husbands to wives.[5] A husband was to be a spiritual leader to his wife, no less than to his servants. The social supremacy of husbands over wives was fixed in law, most spectacularly in the 1352 Statute of Treason, in which a wife who killed her husband was classified as a petty traitor. Legally, when a wife married her husband, she ceased to exist as a civil person, a *femme sole*, and became the legal fiction, *femme couvert*. In Elizabeth Fowler's words: "a marriage contract establishes an agency relationship in which the wife undergoes a degree of 'civil death'" called *coverture*.[6] Coverture demonstrates neatly how the law can be a useful measure of culture. A *femme couvert* was a fiction, medieval society knew, and it demonstrated this knowledge by ensuring that even a wife could be tried for a felony. Women could, of course, commit all manner of crimes physically, but they could not be tried for all the manner of offenses they could commit. The overwhelming status of the husband meant that a civil trespass on the part of the wife would result in a legal invocation of coverture: "civil death does not mean a loss of all power to intend or act but the fiction of such loss and therefore a corresponding degree of powerlessness and of immunity within a particular community and a particular jurisdiction."[7] If a wife committed a civil offense, therefore, both she and her husband would be tried. In the eyes of the law a wife could not commit an offense regarding money, even though she could certainly physically do so. Moreover, since this peculiar binocular vision pertained to wives, we must look for it in discussions about servants as well. Just as wives could sometimes be compelled to do their husbands' dirty work because of their relative immunity to the law, so could servants be, when they were protected by the superior power of their lords and insulated by reciprocities of responsibility and protection.

In one medieval sense, all of these unequal relationships (lord-retainer, master-servant, husband-wife) were based on "maintenance." Maintenance is a medieval word, and not always one of disapproval, as the *Middle English Dictionary* reminds us: for the English from the late fourteenth century onward, maintenance meant supportive behavior, whether for the good, or for the bad.[8] After all, maintenance—strictly speaking, being provided or providing the wherewithal to live—was the business of just about everyone. Everyone sought some level of maintenance from others, and in turn, everyone provided some level of support to someone else (often many others). Moreover, lest we forget, "wherewithal to live" was far from simply economic, but involved social networks as well, as the roots of "affine" and "affinity" in the Latin verbs of attachment remind us. Mutual respect and obligation, and sometimes genuine affection, were recognized as characterizing all these relations: informal, formal, and kin.[9] Contemporaries used a similar range of terminology to describe relationships between lord and man, kinship, and more informal sorts of relations between social superiors and inferiors.

The definition of maintenance that has captured the attention of medievalists, and that loomed large for medieval English writers, was a more negative one, however. Throughout this book, I will trace positive maintenance relationships through literature, especially the bond between lord and knight, and even the related relationship between husbands and wives. In the end, however, I will come to concentrate on the very specific type of maintenance, so overwhelming to medieval authors, known as "maintenance-at-law." Technically defined, maintenance-at-law was the supporting of another's lawsuit for one's own benefit. We can see how the ideology of service might create a grey area between the demands of service and maintenance-at-law. As coverture and female felons, maintenance-at-law as a legal offense revealed a cultural tension: lords, masters, and husbands had responsibilities to support their men, servants, and wives, but doing so could be maintenance-at-law. Therefore, maintenance-at-law may not have been intrinsically wrong, but served as a reminder that the demands placed on either party of a service relationship could be pushed too far.

Now, obviously, medieval retinues were not the Mob, but the Mob certainly practiced a modern form of medieval maintenance-at-law. This illustration helps point to why the topic came to fascinate me, nevertheless. No literary critic has yet considered how a culture suffused with service relationships, or with maintenance as a positive phenomenon, manifested such preoccupations in its literature. At the same time, while historians have examined lordship and patronage with a microscope for decades now, using a full range of military, governmental, and estate documentation, they have failed to take literary examples into systematic account.[10] Affinities comprised of indentured retainers usually contained solely upper-class men, but the ideology of service was practiced by men and women farther down the social scale as well, and I argue that anxieties about these relationships surface in those two special cultural markers: literature and law.

What a consideration of maintenance in literature uncovers is a sophisticated understanding of personal autonomy that is quite alien to our modern No Means No culture.[11] Modern Western culture is obsessed with personal freedom; yet, it appears medieval literary audiences would find the same exercise of freedom not only emotionally unsettling, but socially dangerous, and even personally disrespectful. As medieval Christians, these audiences knew that they had been created by God with free will. However, at the same time, they gave up various degrees of autonomy to a range of deeply respected social institutions: clerical orders, marriage, and service relationships including maintenance. To return to the Mob analogy, your brother *could* disobey the order from his boss; technically, he did have the agency to do so. On another level, however, he had given up part of that autonomy to choose for himself when he joined the Mob: saying "no" was not always an option.

But why concentrate on maintenance per se? Why emphasize the lord–retainer relationship? The answer lies in its contemporary weight and issues related to the modern notion of class. The bond between a lord and his retainer was highly regarded in medieval society. More menial servants existed than retainers, but the relative social status of lord and retainer ensured that medieval society would esteem this bond uniquely. Medieval authors employed the husband–wife and master–servant analogies for their ubiquity: they exploited the lord-retainer relationship for its nobility. Moreover, because of the status of the lords involved in lord-retainer relationships, criticism of this dynamic could be dangerously political.

While literary critics have done relatively little exploration of maintenance, historians have studied it for decades. No discussion of maintenance and the relationship between lords and their men could be written without reference to the seminal work of K.B. McFarlane.[12] While well aged at this point, McFarlane's work still succinctly lays out, in a relatively uncontroversial way, some facts about the crucial service relationship between lords and "lesser" men of the lower nobility or upper gentry. McFarlane recognized the role of military service in the origins of retaining, but insisted that peace time demands on retainers were even more important socially than their service in war. McFarlane argued that retainers existed on a continuum of levels of service that included regular household servants, and that "it would obviously be unwise to draw a clear line between one group and another."[13] Even relatives, near and distant, figured into these networks.[14] These connections established and helped to support a lord's "worship": as McFarlane defines it, his "standing among his fellow noblemen."[15] The networks' "active presence and support endowed [the lord] with the influence through which he could promote both their worship and his own."[16] Clearly, for McFarlane, service was a two-way street, and each side bore responsibilities to the other.

In looking more closely at some of these terms, more recent scholarship can guide us. In his survey of royal affinities from Edward III through Henry IV, Chris Given-Wilson offers a useful general definition of an affinity, "the servants, retainers, and other followers of a lord," and he asserts that the affinity "was the most important political grouping in medieval society."[17] J.M.W. Bean includes estate officials as nominal members of the household: indeed, according to Bean, local administrators, such as receivers, stewards, and bailiffs, were key members of retinues.[18] Given-Wilson identifies two groups who primarily made up the king's affinity: intimates and those bound to regular service by regular wages formed an inner group, while a second, larger group consisted of more independent men who "were not employed by [the king] on a full-time basis."[19] Given-Wilson identifies this second group as the king's "retinue" and sees a split in noble affinities similar to that in the royal affinity, and a similarity between Richard II's retaining practices and those of Henry IV.

In the end, these historians' evidence points to a flexible definition of retaining, including formally indentured members, periodically resident officials, and household servants. Indeed, for Christine Carpenter, the wide gentry networks of kin, neighbor, and friends could at times appear nearly parallel to the retinues of the gentry's greater neighbors, the nobility: "in a sense the greater gentry also were lords of affinities, an essential connecting-point in the ascending hierarchy from neighborhood to region to country. It was through their connections, and to a lesser extent through those of the middling gentry, that the influence of the [noble] affinity would percolate through a region."[20] Affinities and retinues were made up of men at a range of social levels, who shared a range of ties to their lord, both personal and contractual. Some profited from permanent remuneration for regular service, and some did not, but nevertheless, still benefited from their relationship with their lord. The lord–retainer relationship was a noble form of the master–servant relationship: they existed on a continuum.

Bean argues that indentures of retinue, annuities, and livery all developed from household practice, and the range of rewards a retainer could hope for in remuneration of his past and future service varied considerably. A late medieval retainer could gain "tangible benefits in the form of, for example, money payments or perquisites through membership of his lord's household; but he would also expect to enjoy his lord's favor in a less tangible way—for example, support and influence in the courts of law or assistance in securing offices from the Crown."[21] In his treatment of the Lancastrian affinity, Simon Walker claims that "the strength of the [...] tie lay, not in the pre-eminence of the lord, but in an expectation of mutual benefit, a community of aim, and outlook between the contracting parties."[22] There is much to this assertion that we shall see reinforced throughout this book: the centrality of mutual benefit and responsibility between lord and man, and the notion of contract, even without the legal instrument. Beyond the retainers, there were a mass of others receiving annuities for "good service, done in the past and to be done in the future."[23] Each segment of this network vied with the others for the range of riches in John of Gaunt's gift: not simply indentures of retinue, and annuities, Gaunt also had "land, money, offices, wardships, leases, timber, venison…benefices, corrodies, and pardon of crimes" as well as less tangible, but perhaps more valuable "countenance, support, and protection."[24]

This is not to say that the medieval English situation was static. Bean charts a move very generally from lordship to patronage during the later Middle Ages, and he characterizes the change thusly:

> the term "lordship" involves a situation in which the relationships between a lord and his follower depend on the lord's use of wealth which is his own. A patron, on the other hand, while he may use his own resources, will also assist his man in a looser way that involves, not his tangible assets, but the influence he wields.[25]

As Walker puts it, "the duke [of Lancaster] turned from fees to favour as the instrument of his lordship."[26]

Lawyers were a special group in a number of ways, and they exemplified the category of servant who had multiple allegiances. As does Carpenter, Michael Hicks emphasizes that there was a trickle-down of practices: nobles retained gentry, and gentry retained those below them on the social scale.[27] The loyalties of all of these individuals could be split. A steward might have more than one employer, but so might a lawyer, and one could pay rent to more than one landlord as well. Walker posits that since Gaunt retained men for specific tasks, as long as those tasks continued to be performed, a Lancastrian retainer could in good conscience contract with other lords, and he gives lawyers and estate officials as specific examples.[28] Loyalty remained a valued characteristic, and Hicks examines how practicing it led to complex negotiations among lords and men with multiple allegiances. Such complexities were usually unremarkable to contemporaries, argues Hicks. Walker closes with a reminder that sounds throughout the present book: "lordship was never a magnate monopoly; it was delegated, appropriated, mediatized, and diffused throughout a society far more complex in its workings than the starkly contractual terms of an indenture of retainer suggest."[29]

Legal personnel worked inside an ethical gray area, always close to maintenance-at-law. Most historians use this narrow definition of maintenance to reference corruption of the legal system. McFarlane points out that "laboring" juries, sheriffs, and others, was a form of embracery, or bribery, and more common than "maintenance, by which I mean attempts to overawe the court by the presence of armed men."[30] More recently, Hicks reflects the influence of the new legal history in noting that in many cases, such activity was considered legal behavior.[31]

Legal historians and their opinions concerning maintenance-at-law deserve special attention, and several "new" legal historians have weighed in on the topic. J.G. Bellamy considers how the findings of political historians, and the preliminary work by social historians, intersected with the legal tradition:

> The roots of crime lie more in social institutions and attitudes than in the personalities of the individuals who compose society. The bane of late medieval England above all else was the widespread maintenance that was practiced, that is to say the illegal support which magnates offered to a lesser man's suit by word, writing, or physical deed.[32]

This is the foundation on which the present book rests. Bellamy connects social institutions with legal institutions, and sees maintenance-at-law as existing in both worlds, social and legal.

Yet, thanks to the work of scholars in the intervening years, by 1989, Bellamy had modulated his position concerning maintenance. We can see, in the preceding quote, how Bellamy employs the modifier "illegal" to describe the maintenance that concerns him. In *Bastard Feudalism and the Law*, Bellamy recognizes the relativism inherent in our modern understanding of this practice as "bad." Certainly there was outcry against it, but in the more recent book, Bellamy admits that the line between what was acceptable and what was going too far appears rather gray to our modern sensibilities. He notes how contemporary definitions of the legal term emphasize "maintain[ing] malicious enterprises": but, I add that we might ask ourselves who got to define "malicious."[33] Bellamy explains how the line between laboring a jury, that is, giving them information about "correct" interpretation of events, and encouraging them to vote based on their consciences, could shade into maintenance easily, and a losing party in a case might think so, especially.[34]

For Bellamy, the list of expectations a lord had of retainers was extensive, flexible, and often included legal activity. "His retainers and associates" might be expected to do any of the following: witness contracts and other legal transactions, be his executors, labor juries for the lord or another retainer or associate, labor on the lord's behalf for parliamentary elections, or participate in out-of-court settlements.[35] Members of a lord's retinue might also be required to assist in overawing local courts, aiding the lord in physically regaining land lost, and financially benefitting the lord through their gifts to him.[36] While this highlights the bind in which retainers of higher degree could find themselves, the "associates" could easily be lawyers, who would be hired (in modern terms, "retained") to do precisely these activities as part of their professional duties. The line between "bad" maintenance in the form of embracery and hiring a lawyer could be relative indeed.

Anthony Musson characterizes "new legal history" as historiography that "questions the specialisation and discrete

compartmentalisation that has largely characterised its prede-
cessors, aiming instead at a more holistic and interdisciplinary
interpretation."[37] Bellamy's step in 1989 was a characteristically
cautious one, and I hope I follow his example. As a critic, my
strengths lie in textual interpretation, rather than statistical analysis, and therefore, this book will rest on literature and textual historical documentation. This book takes part in a dialog with new
legal history. The ways the lord/retainer relationship and its analogs
echoed throughout medieval English society can be illuminated,
read, and described when a literary critic examines the literary
and cultural (including legal) evidence surrounding these practices.
How could a social feature as respected as retaining be absent from
literary products? Yet, no literary critic has sought for it across the
literature of late medieval England. Not usually interested in literature as a significant historical source, while studying relationships
between lords and men, and masters and servants, historians have
essayed into literary territory as far as the letter collections, and we
shall turn to these next, in chapter 2.

Chapter 2 provides contemporary insight into these terms and
relationships through a short examination of fifteenth-century letter collections. While traditional historians such as McFarlane and
recent historians such as David Gary Shaw and the literary critic
Raluca Radulescu have mined these sources, the letter collections
remain relatively underutilized, and letters are usually relegated to
providing color to studies whose primary sources lie elsewhere.[38]
Here they will furnish contemporary accounts of different sorts of
service relationships, and will begin to demonstrate some ways in
which relationships between lords and their men were similar to
those between men and their own servants: everyone was maintained within a social fabric.

If criticizing lords was potentially hazardous, one might discuss
marriage in medieval literature with relative impunity. As we shall
see in chapter 3 , a medieval author who wished to explore some of
the negative sides of retaining might choose to write instead about
husbands and wives, an analogous relationship, and one enjoying,

or plagued by, a long tradition of satire and criticism. Chapter 3 considers the relationships between husbands and wives in literature, particularly during a crisis that put the legal fictions couples inhabited under extreme stress, rape. Late medieval England demonstrated awareness of the problems civil death could cause in changing legislation surrounding rape, and this awareness surfaces in the literature in startling ways. Feminist critics have noted the extraordinary number of rapes in Middle English literature, particularly in the Chaucerian canon, and chapter 3 seeks to set the tendency to write about rape within one possible social and legal context, coverture. Rape forced medieval legal officials and writers to consider the degree to which autonomy was compromised as the responsibilities of service clashed with the sense of autonomy modern readers associate with "free will," particularly in the social, legal, and religious institution of marriage. Chaucer's *Franklin's Tale* provides an example of what coverture looks like in literature, and also introduces some of the logical problems that the coverture system faced when a wife was raped (or threatened with it). I examine texts from the *Wife of Bath's Tale* to the variations on the Lucretia story, and find that each expresses medieval authors' concern with the constraints coverture placed on the autonomy of wives and, perhaps surprisingly, also of husbands. This state of affairs is understandable when we remember that marriage was seen as a type of service relationship, analogous to that between a lord and a retainer. Authors make it clear that these stories suggest ways in which men in service relationships face similar constraints.

Authors choosing to describe the lord–retainer relationship outright had to tread carefully. Chapter 4 examines literary texts for explicit examples of relationships between lords and retainers. In Chaucer's corpus, the little-read *Tale of Melibee* reveals a lord of retainers (and lawyers) in the titular character. Lady Meed, a character in *Piers Plowman*, demonstrates in literature the legal analogy between marriage as a social institution and service, and unquestionably, Meed has a retinue and acts as a lord of men. Hidden in his *Fall of Princes*, Lydgate's brief Arthuriad describes the Round Table knights as a retinue, and connects their responsibilities to those of knightly societies of his own day.

Chapter 5 closes the book by considering the relationships between masters and a particular category of servants: lawyers. Educated, and sometimes relatively wealthy, lawyers were servants, and sometimes retainers, whose relationship with the legal system put special strain on the traditional relational structures this book examines. One of the most contentious arenas in which the tension between autonomy and service could be seen was the law. Gower's *Mirour de l'Omme* and *Vox Clamantis* both expose a developing sense that legal professionals and the equity of the law suffered when service was involved. The question began to become whether a lawyer's lord was a man or the law itself. Which institutions or individuals had the right to constrain a lawyer's autonomy? Hoccleve's *Regiment of Princes* includes references to his own struggles with this problem as a clerk of the Privy Seal. While Gower seeks primarily to map out the problem in detail, Hoccleve's personal circumstances force him to suggest a solution. It is with personal circumstances that I will begin, with the letter collections in chapter 2.

CHAPTER 2

MAINTAINING A FAMILY

It is clear from the preceding chapter that "bad" maintenance differed little from other, acceptable practices. Historians may split hairs over terminology, but generally agree that service relationships existed on a continuum including a wide range of people engaged in diverse relationships. Before turning to the literature in the remaining chapters, in the following pages I will use a documentary source, letter collections, to explore how medieval people themselves discussed a variety of service relationships. The dividing line between "good" and "bad" maintenance appears complicated to these fifteenth-century people, many of whom were negotiating the demands of multiple allegiances discussed in chapter 1. As we shall see, lord-retainer and the less noble master-servant relationships were often linked to bad maintenance in these documents. Nevertheless, it would appear that what medieval people saw as bad maintenance reflected personal bias and perspective as much as it did actual deviation in practice from the cultural norm.

As with the literature explored in later chapters, this chapter will concentrate on exemplary moments, case studies, to illustrate its point. To make these case studies more viable as sources, I will concentrate on the Paston, Stonor, and Plumpton letter collections that include exemplars from the 1450s and 1460s only. This will demonstrate how letter writers from several families discussed various relationships over a narrow range of years. None of the letters are "private" as we would think of it today. Rather, they are business correspondence between gentry men and women and their partners, servants, and lords. Preserved thanks to their usefulness as evidence during specific litigation over land, these letters may be difficult to use statistically, yet as windows into a culture and when supported by historiography such as we considered in chapter 1, the letters shine.

The Pastons are the best known of the gentry families whose fifteenth- and sixteenth-century letter collections survive. An East Anglian family, their recent rise into the gentle classes was thanks to a lawyer's savvy. The occasion that created the need for preserving these letters was the disputed will of a local knight, Sir John Falstaff. The Pastons had been on good terms with Falstaff, perhaps too good for the comfort of the other local families, as trouble began when the Pastons claimed that Falstaff had left a number of important properties to them on his deathbed. Struggle over the Falstaff properties, in court and out of it, lasted for decades.

The Stonors, a gentry family based in the Thames valley, also founded its gentility on the law in person of a judge in the fourteenth century. The family negotiated the troubled political waters of Richard II's reign, the Lancastrian takeover, and the Wars of the Roses through a blend of luck and cautious refusal to side too staunchly with any one party. It was not until 1500 that a dispute over inheritance erupted that provided the impetus to archive and preserve the letters we now have. Christine Carpenter, the Stonor letters' most recent editor, argues forcefully that in many ways, the Stonors were more representative of a greater number of gentry families than the Pastons.[1] Carpenter notes that the household members were considered to be members of the family, and this should remind us how the culture of maintenance went both down and up the social hierarchy, as well as how service was linked with the family.[2] Looking upward, family connections linked the Stonors to Thomas Chaucer and the Beauforts, and William de la Pole, Duke of Suffolk. Thomas II Stonor, the individual about whom we will read below, participated in the social and political life of his locality in ways normative for the head of a powerful gentry family. Serving as MP, JP, and sheriff, he avoided the skirmishes of the Wars of the Roses when he could, and seems to have stuck closely to his lord, George Neville, Archbishop of York.

If the Stonors were more characteristic of the gentry as a whole than the Pastons, the Plumptons may fit the militaristic, litigious, grasping stereotype best.[3] First noted as well-off in the eleventh century, the Plumptons were knighted for all of the thirteenth, fourteenth, and fifteenth centuries. Hailing from Yorkshire, the family's proximity to the Marches of the Scottish border necessitated greater military involvement than either the Stonors or the Pastons experienced. Moreover, thanks to a base in Yorkshire, the Plumptons had a long history of sponsorship by the powerful Percy family. Indeed, William Plumpton was an estate steward for the Percies, and as such was one of the estate officials discussed in the previous chapter. Like Stonor and Paston, he also served as JP, MP, and sheriff. The ties to the Percies left the Plumptons more involved in the fifteenth-century political upheavals than either of the other two families. Loyalty to the Percy cause in the 1450s explains why William Plumpton was fighting a losing battle to maintain order in his stewardship, and why he was not fully clear of the treason allegations following the battle of Towton (1461) until 1464.

Surprisingly, given how much the Plumptons appear to be "classic" retainers, the inheritance dispute that occasioned the preservation of the letters was brought about by the scion of the family himself. When William Plumpton's clandestine marriage was upheld and ratified in 1468, it guaranteed the lands he had settled on his son by that marriage, effectively disinheriting his two daughters by a previous marriage, as well as their powerful husbands. This shockingly self-centered act had earlier precedent.[4] As Wilcock puts it: "Sir William Plumpton himself caused men to shift their allegiance [away from him] owing to his blatant self-promotion, land-grabbing, unfair wielding of authority, and violence of his men.... There is no doubt...that Sir William did cause traditional Lancastrian loyalties in the Knaresborough area to be undermined."[5] If Paston characterizes the litigious gentry, and Stonor the pacifistic gentry, then William Plumpton illustrates the militaristic, criminous gentryman who used the position granted him by his lord to promote himself before other local interests, including his own family members. The dramatic events mentioned here take place well outside the ambit of this chapter, though, and so here I will concentrate on several letters from the 1460s that illustrate service binding William Plumpton.

Coming to an Accord: Maintenance in Out of Court Settlements

The Pastons provide us with good example of how ties of lordship and kinship could all come under tension when the law came into the picture.[6] Originating in a debate between Elizabeth Clere and William Stewardson over a piece of property, the conflict escalated to include alleged threats, kidnapping, beatings, and extortion. The feud continued unresolved for years, despite processes in a range of courts including the manor court of Ormesby, King's Bench, and the Court of Chancery. It would appear that the demands of service relationships aggravated the "vareaunce" between Elizabeth Clere and the Stewardsons that led to the exchanges between Thomas, Lord Scales, John Paston I, and Elizabeth Clere preserved in these letters.[7] The interlocking, and sometimes conflicting, set of obligations that this small cast of characters struggle to fulfill would have been familiar to anyone back in Chaucer's day.

Richmond dates the dispute to about 1451, based on court documents; the letters that seem to refer to these events are dated by month and day, but not by year. Nevertheless, they must date to before Scales' death in 1460. If Clere's letter to John Paston I (600) outlines events occurring during the initial wave of offense-taking, it should date to about 1451. Litigation was initiated on both sides, and lasted from 1451–54, and I suggest that the related letters (592–94 and perhaps 597) date within this time period. In notes to each letter, Davis connects 592 and 593, and 594 with 600. Now, as we will see below, even if 592 and 593 do not refer to the dispute of 594 and 600 their language is illustrative of the language used in the resolution to such disputes; therefore, these letters will be discussed at length below.

Clere's letter to Paston for advice recounts an altercation taking place after an Easter Vigil mass.[8] Stewardson, one of Lord Scales' men, approached Clere very publicly at church, "among þe more part of al þe parisch."[9] This was a sacred venue and solemn religious

moment that placed restrictions on Clere's responses to her antag-
onist: she tells Paston that "I seide if it had be another day I schuld
a rehersed many mo thyngges."[10] Easter Vigil is the last possible
moment in the Church year to cleanse a spotted conscience before
the highly solemn occasion of Easter. The presence of her tenants
and parishioners was in her favor, since she says they would support
her claims, but due to the solemnity of the day, she was unable to
make her accusations as freely as she would have liked.

Seemingly in the spirit of Easter Vigil, Stewardson "preide [Clere]
to be his good mastras, *and* wold put hym-self in [her] rewle."[11] But
Clere would have none of this posturing. At this point, she voiced
her desire for peace, or at least cessation of violence, but also made
her demand for explicitly financial satisfaction. "I lete hym wete,"
Clere told Paston, "þat I was in charite, for I wold to hym no
bodily harm."[12] Charity here is explicitly linked to refraining from
physical violence, but as Clere continues, peace for her requires
financial compensation: "if a theef come and robbed me...on the
to day and come and asked for-yifness on the tothyr day, were
it reson þat I schuld for-yeve it without satisfaccioun," she asked,
implying an answer in the negative.[13]

When Stewardson agreed that one ought not forgive a repen-
tant thief without financial compensation, the argument devolved
further into trading allegations of slander. According to Clere,
Stewardson used this event as an excuse to "noyse" and "slaunder"
her, which Clere was "wers plesed with-all þan with ony mony þat
I have spent, and as for þat I yaf litel force of."[14] Stewardson later
denied the charges of slander against Clere, and at this point in the
narrative, Clere launched into her account of events that seem to be
at the root of the dispute, and they include service and bad maintenance at a number of levels.

The very public location of the dispute is important; who had
spoken truthfully had legal ramifications since lawsuits were ongo-
ing.[15] Clere claimed that she was acting legally in sending servants
to take possession of a small property to which Stewardson also
believed he had the rights. She asserted that Stewardson had accused
her men falsely of beating him, and had made the accusation before
Stewardson's lord, Scales, "vp-on which vntrewe langgage his

maister hath take an accion ageyn me *and* my men."[16] While this situation seems to fit the narrow definition of maintenance, in that Scales was upholding another's suit in court, Clere's concern here is hardly a quibble about who brought the suit. She is angry simply because the wrongful suit exists at all. Indeed, Clere seems unsurprised that Stewardson's "maister" had taken up the case. After all, Scales was just practicing good lordship. It was Stewardson who was manipulating the system inappropriately here, to Clere's mind.

After "many crafty wordes" Stewardson admits that he had spoken falsely. "Þis I bad my tenauntes schuld recorden," Clere recounts, "for al þat þat was seid was seid openly among þe more part of al þe parisch."[17] Thus, Stewardson's lies, now publicly confessed, had embroiled his master in a false lawsuit, placing his lord at legal risk for bringing a wrongful suit to court.

Despite believing that "for his mayntenaunce [Stewardson] schal fare þe worse," Clere herself asks advice of her council who themselves have ties to more than one lord.[18] John Heydon and William Jenny, and we find, Paston himself, have ties to both Clere and Scales. Perhaps in an attempt to get better counsel from him, Clere reinforces kinship ties in her letter to Paston, calling him and herself "cosyn" several times, a term that referred to a close relationship, although not necessary close blood kinship.[19] She expresses frustration with her council's multiple ties, calling Heydon, Jenny, "and mo of my counsell" "double to [Scales] and to me."[20] The sense of "double" here is tricky: the easiest reading is simply that these men served on both councils. However, the MED also attests to meanings for "double" suggesting duplicity.[21] So either Jenny and Heydon are problematic counselors because they serve on opposing councils, or they are out for themselves, and neither's counsel is completely trustworthy. Around the time of these letters, Jenny tried to maintain a respectful relationship with Paston: in an apologetic Letter 580 Jenny reminds Paston that "my service is redy to you at alle tymys as ye shewe me gret cause to doo you service."[22] Certainly, both Jenny and Heydon fended for themselves well: in 1460 Jenny became a close associate of Paston's nemesis Yelverton in the Falstaff land debacle that kept the Pastons busy for so many years, and by 1463 he was a serjeant-at-law and therefore a member of a select group of lawyers at the national level. Heydon was cagey enough for Paston to say of him in 1465 that "yf he do oght therin he doyth it closely, as he ys wont to doo, and wayshyth hys hondys therof as Pylate dyde," and Heydon shows up frequently in the letters, usually having caused a disturbance with his men.[23] Nevertheless, despite his own "doubleness" to Scales, Clere still trusts Paston to give her good advice about "what answer is best to yeve, my worschep saved."[24]

Indeed, for Clere, maintenance seemed to be an institution that was as ethical as the uses to which it was put. Although Clere had friends who "labor" for her as well, and a "counsell lerned," she said to Stewardson that "his maister schuld leve his mayntenaunce, wherof I schuld haue right good suerté or ellys we schuld not go thorgh esyly."[25] The "learned council" was a characteristic of gentry and noble households of the later middle ages, and usually included those with legal knowledge.[26] Given his relationship with several members of Clere's counsel, Scales' maintenance puts Clere at a disadvantage in these negotiations, and in this letter, she reminds Paston of his positions as learned counsel and kin, in an attempt to even the score. Clere's own practices illustrate how loyalty and preferential treatment was expected from allies; therefore, retainers with ties to multiple lords could easily find themselves between a rock and a hard place. The relationship between Paston and Scales and Paston and Clere differed in degree, if that, but not in kind.

The letters between Scales and Paston give further insight into the service culture referenced in Clere's letter. They all demonstrate how the difference between good and bad maintenance could be purely a matter of perspective. In letter 594, from Lord Scales to his retainer, John Paston I, Scales identifies William Stewardson as his servant.[27] Stewardson and Clere were in dispute, and as a good lord should, Scales was using his network to attempt to defuse the situation, asking Paston to "intrete the said Elizabeth to such appointment as the brynger of þis letter shal informe you of."[28] Consideration of the legal implications of "appointement" is interesting: the MED lists three different definitions for "appointement." The first definition, "a formal agreement," is the most general, while the second and third have legal resonance: "an agreement between hostile parties," and "the fixing of a date for official business."[29]

The rest of the letter is full of reminders of Paston's duty to Scales as a retainer, who also is a "right trusty and welbeloued frend."[30] Scales reminds his man of the mutual obligations binding the two of them: Scales asks Paston to "do your trewe dilligence in þis mater as ye wyll I do for you in any thyng ye may haue ado in þis cuntré."[31] As Walker noted of both John of Gaunt's retaining and Henry IV's, "one good turn deserved another."[32] Scales' formulation also recalls the local nature of the powers he could bring to bear on Paston's behalf. Locally based, too, is Paston's interest in Elizabeth Clere; the Cleres and the Pastons were fast friends, close enough that Elizabeth could loan the Pastons considerable sums of money without rancor on either side.[33]

Letter 594 dates to August 31, but Scales' interest, and his preparations for the "appointement" may be attested in other letters as well. In letters 592 and 593, Scales sets up and then responds to a meeting between "a squier of myn called Elyngham" and Paston.[34] In 592, of July 18, Scales simply alerts Paston that Elingham is on his way, and that Paston ought to listen to Elingham's message from Scales. 593 dates to August 3, and in it, Scales refers to a meeting between Elingham and Paston and asks Paston to "assigne such a day as you liketh best, so þat it be with-jnne this viij dayes."[35] Davis suggests that 592 and 593 are related to 594, and all relate to different attempts to resolve the dispute that lasted for years. If the beginnings of the "vareaunce" were in the spring at Easter time, the wording of 594 suggests a formal request for Paston's participation in a resolution of a situation about which he undoubtedly already knew.

Service culture suffuses these letters, and we see easily that the practice was weighed in the writers' minds based upon the uses to which it was put. Maintenance could be perceived as good or bad simply depending on whether the speaker's side was winning. Multiple allegiances to lords, servants, retainers, and kin dog many of these decisions. Service was a fact of life, and people could use it as a mechanism for social stability, or they could impose on it to assist in unbalancing a local situation.

Good Lordship: Responsibilities to Servants and Neighbors

Unlike the litigious Pastons, the Stonors maintained their properties centered in the Thames valley fairly placidly. This makes the well-documented dispute between Thomas Stonor and his bailiff, John Frende, and Richard Fortescue (brother to the chief justice) unusual in the long run of Stonor correspondence.[36] In short, litigation commenced over an assault on Stonor and his bailiff Frende by Fortescue and his men at a property far from Stonor's other holdings, and one he rarely visited. As Carpenter has surmised: "it seems that for ensuring the security of some of their more far-flung properties the family was reliant primarily on associations made through lordship rather than on their own efforts to secure local friends."[37] As with the Clere-Stewardson dispute, multiple attempts in and out of court were made to resolve the issue, and in the case of Frende, we have evidence of the intimidation retinues could cause for retainers far from their lords, as well as the responsibilities retainers felt their lords had toward them.

The first two letters seem to predate the assault on Frende and Stonor: Carpenter dates them to spring of 1462. Although clearly a professional letter, the first order of business for Frende in Letter 63 is to determine "where [Stonor] wil come in to Devenshire to abide."[38] He describes a local situation in which Stonor's absence is beginning to cost Stonor his good name and reputation as a good lord in Devonshire. Stonor's tenants felt forced to submit to Fortescue's wishes, because although Stonor promised to visit, he "kepe not [his] promise at no tyme."[39] There are two implied accusations here. One, that Stonor was not a man of his word, was serious enough that it should have prompted swift action.[40] The other accusation explores the mutual responsibility between a lord and his tenants and servants: if they were to be loyal to him, he had to support and protect their bodies and their interests. Stonor was not doing this, Frende claims.

Letter 64 seems to postdate 63, and is far more insistent than the last: "[a list of perpetrators, and servants of Fortescue] mauneseth me dayly, and put me in suche fere of my lyffe [...] that I dere not go to cherche ne to chepyng." Frende here refers to two responsibilities of his employer's: to ensure that Frende is a good Christian, and that his goods can be taken to market. Furthermore, Frende details a slander case, wherein the men associated with Fortescue's servants in the previous letter claim that Frende has sent men to steal from one of them. Frende insists that the slanderous accusation is a lie. Frende repeats his pleas for aid, and aid specifically in the form of an extended visit by Stonor to make his presence more strongly felt in that locality. Again, we see that perspective is important to consider. Fortescue is "making his presence strongly felt in that locality" as a lord should, and as Stonor should: it is only Frende's status as an estate official of the less present lord that makes Fortescue a threatening prospect. Without that physical presence, Frende reports that public fame is moving against Stonor: "thay putteth in uterance daily that we schalbe undowe, for ye nel never come to helpe us."[41] Finally, Frende reports that one of the crew is heading to London to begin legal process against him. "Also but ye come and defende me," Frende reminds Stonor, in his coup de grace, "I wille do the service no lengher, for I may not ne dernot."[42] The mutual responsibility between lord and retainer is here explicit: Frende has done his duty to remind Stonor of his, and if Stonor once again refuses that responsibility, then their relationship is at an end.

On May 10, 1462, Stonor made good on his promises, and visited the Devonshire estates, and on this day he and John Frende were allegedly assaulted by Fortescue.[43] At this point in the dispute, the letters shift from those between Stonor and his bailiff to those between Stonor and his lawyer, including copies of legal bills, and provide more insight into relations between lords and their employees, kin, and retainers. Thomas Mulle, Stonor's lawyer, refers to him as "ryght worshipfull Brother," referring to their status as in-laws.[44] Most likely, Mulle refers to an arbitration over this dispute in 1463 in his report that "the Award of Devonshir is not such as I wold it wer," and expresses both professional and familial concern that the award was not favorable to Stonor.[45] By 1466, the arbitration agreement had been entirely broken, and litigation resumed in King's Bench, and then Chancery.

Making good on his threat, Frende appears to have ceased acting as Stonor's bailiff in Devonshire after 1465. In 1466, John Yeme is writing to Thomas Stonor as bailiff and he complains of Fortescue's violence and overwhelming control over the local courts in Letter 81. Fortescue's retainers have forced Yeme into court needlessly, "and y hadde myche labur to gete me a weye."[46] Indeed, Yeme invokes the legal rhetoric of "feloniously laying in wait" when he recounts that "Ric. Fortescu ffaryth ffowle...and layyth his men yn awayte to murder me when y was laste atte Ermyngton atte Corte."[47] Fortescue's influence over local courts explains his plans, as Yeme claims the reason Fortescue went so far as to plan to murder him was "y wolde notte suffry hym to have his yntente at Plympton Corte."[48] Yeme goes on to describe how Fortescue's power at the court of Tremonton was so great that he could pursue cases in an idiosyncratic manner because of his retainers' presence there. Fortescue had the power in the locality to "overawe" courts, and is willing to use this power to push out the weak lord, Stonor. While it would appear that Fortescue was acting beyond acceptable practice, once again we see how the line between bad and good maintenance could become blurred. As we saw in chapter 1, overawing the court was considered improper, but only in degree. One's party *should* awe the court, and Stonor's absence was simultaneously handicapping his worship and creating a power vacuum that Fortescue was more than willing to fill.

Two documents related to Chancery suits again demonstrate the narrow line between good and bad maintenance. One is a copy of Frende's bill in Chancery, and another appears to be a draft of a suit Stonor prepared, but did not bring against Fortescue in Chancery. Both list infractions by Fortescue against the two plaintiffs, as well as others in their care. Stonor's draft concentrates on Fortescue's obstruction of justice through his failure to carry out the arbitration agreement, and how this failure harmed not only Stonor, but many people in the area with ties to Stonor, a wide-ranging group the draft calls "welwyllers."[49] The "welwyllers" show up as aggrieved parties a few times in the draft, for as Stonor claims, Fortescue "suyth and avexyth divers pepill for love of me...to my grete charge."[50] Frende, in particular, is brought up as a distressed party.[51] By taking up others' suits in court, Stonor is nearly engaged in bad maintenance. However, by bringing these suits, Stonor is finally accepting the responsibility he bore for looking out for his men in Devonshire: this is good maintenance.

Letter 80 is a copy of the bill Frende brought before the Chancellor in 1466 complaining that the previous December, Fortescue forcibly took Frende into custody, and imprisoned him in Fortescue's house until Frende paid him five marks. While the florid account of the offense owes much to the rhetoric of Chancery bills, just as Frende's claims of poverty likely do, there is plenty of evidence for our investigation in the material. Technically, there were two classes of offenses with which Chancery dealt: cases whose progress or decision had been influenced by maintenance, and cases that did not fall under the purview of the common law. Frende admits in his bill that his false imprisonment should have been sued in the common law of King's Bench, but argues that his poverty prevented him from pursuing this option. What goes unspoken is the power that Fortescue clearly held in that part of Devonshire, a power that extended to the courts, as Yeme's letter contends, and Stonor's draft bill illustrates. We have seen in Letters 63 and 64 how tenuous was Stonor's authority in the area: to take the suit to Chancery rather than King's Bench may have been an admission (although perhaps a tardy one) of the very real power vacuum that Stonor's absence from his Devonshire estate had caused, and an admission that Fortescue had been quick to fill the void. At Chancery then, closer to Oxfordshire than Devonshire, Stonor may have hoped his authority held more sway than Fortescue's. Both Stonor and his lawyer Mulle appear in person as Frende's pledges for the justice of his case: at last, Stonor was supporting his beleaguered bailiff, and doing so shoulder-to-shoulder with his retained lawyer and brother-in-law.[52] Again, while standing as Frende's pledge was Stonor's responsibility as his employer and lord, it also skirted being maintenance, narrowly defined.

The Chancery and Common Pleas suits between Frende and Fortescue provide a wonderful demonstration of how service relationships moved both down and up the social scale. In a detail that reminds us that neither side was innocent of using the system in their favor, Fortescue points out that it is unfair of Frende to sue him in Chancery for wrongful imprisonment when he is already engaged in a suit in the Court of Common Pleas for the same offense.[53] If Frende's lord Stonor was a retainer of the Archbishop of York who happened to be Chancellor, as Letter 82 suggests, a Chancery suit could have been a very good move, indeed. The Common Pleas case could always be dropped, as we see that it was.[54] Having struggled without the presence of his lord, once having acquired his attention, Frende capitalizes on all available ties of service.[55]

Maintaining Society Well and Ill

It has already been suggested that William Plumpton may have pushed maintenance too far in a self-serving direction, and his son had to deal with the consequences. While these decisions may have been founded in William's personality, due to his location in Yorkshire William Plumpton was perhaps more tightly entangled in service relationships than either Paston or Stonor, and he had to respond to these responsibilities at a time when those very ties pushed him into a national political fracas that neither the Pastons nor Stonors dealt with to the same degree. The Plumptons had been Percy men traditionally, and when the Percies were ousted from regional primacy following the battle of Towton, their title of Earls of Northumberland was handed to their rivals, the Nevilles. This placed William Plumpton, who had fought for the Lancastrian Percies, in a difficult position. We see his conflicts unfold in a short series of letters from his superiors in the difficult 1460s.

The Plumpton correspondence actually begins with a March 13, 1461, letter from Henry VI to Plumpton, an order to collect men for defense of the Lancastrian regime following Edward's March 4 proclamation announcing himself king. Certainly, purveying armed men in defense of the king was a traditional task for the knightly orders, and Plumpton seems to have accepted the directive in due course. In such a tumultuous historical moment, it seems particularly poignant that Henry calls Plumpton "trusty and welbeloved," for although the phrase was formulaic, loyal Plumpton certainly was: we know that his eldest son was killed at Towton, along with their lord, the 3rd Percy Earl of Northumberland.[56]

Following the Yorkist victory at Towton, and Northumberland's death, the Percy estates were divided among their rivals, the Yorkist Nevilles, and we find Nevilles giving orders to Plumpton. Letter 11, dated only to sometime between Towton and Warwick's rebellion (1469) shows Richard Neville, Earl of Warwick and Salisbury, calling Plumpton to heel over a land dispute with one of Warwick's men. He states firmly that Plumpton should wait for an arbitration to determine who had the rights to the property. While this was Warwick's responsibility for his man, it was also an opportunity for him to remind a staunch Lancastrian and Percy retainer that the new order was ready only to accept his quiet obedience.

Letter 17 demonstrates Plumpton, a survivor if there ever was one, trying to make use of the new regime as he had the old. In it, the new Earl of Northumberland, Warwick's brother John Neville, writes to Sir John Mauleverer that Plumpton had complained to Northumberland on behalf of some of his servants who had been threatened by Mauleverer's servants: "Sir William Plumpton, knight, hath sent unto me, and complayneth him that Thomas Wade and Richard Crofty dayly threats to beat or slay his servants...wherefore I desire and pray you to cause the said Thomas and Richard to surcease."[57] Northumberland orders Mauleverer to control his servants better, but also reminds Mauleverer that "if they have any matters against his said servants, lett them complaine unto me therof, and I shall see that they shall have such a remedy, as shall accord with reason."[58] This serves as a reminder that lords functioned as a kind of first tier in the developing criminal justice system. In order to be a "good master," here Plumpton is appealing to a higher authority, even one of an opposing party, on behalf of his men. As much as it may have chagrined Plumpton to recognize Northumberland's local power, he did know that Mauleverer was

Northumberland's man, and that the best route to him was through his lord as Earl of Northumberland, now holding increased responsibility for criminal justice in Yorkshire.[59] A plea such as this letter reveals could be an excellent way to assess a new regime: how partisan was John Neville going to be, now that he was Earl? In other words, was he willing to expand his service network to include those under his power who had fought for the other side in order to preserve the local peace? It appears that the Nevilles were willing, as Plumpton soon regained a portion of his former station, albeit as deputy to Warwick, who occupied a number of Plumpton's former offices.

Plumpton's litigiousness may have been exacerbated by the Wars of the Roses, but its extent may have rivaled that of the Pastons' legal maneuvering. In December of 1469, the same Sir John Mauleverer discussed above said about Plumpton that, "[Plumpton] had sued all the trew men to the king, to my lord [Northumberland], and to him in the forest [a separate jurisdiction in the Forest of Knaresborough], [. . . .]; and that [Mauleverer] shold complaine to the king and to the lords thereof."[60] Once the Yorkists (and therefore the Nevilles) were in power, a man like Mauleverer could extend his pique against Plumpton with more impunity than previously: "[Mauleverer] wold deele with [Plumpton and his men], both be the law and besides the law; and [. . .] wold cutt the clothes notwithstanding."[61] The fact that the slights leveled between Plumpton and Mauleverer, and those between their men, had a history stretching back decades ensured that the tension we see recorded in letters from the nobility to Plumpton and Mauleverer would be mirrored in interactions at a level below the gentrymen as well.

We view these conflicts almost exclusively through a continuous stream of letters to Plumpton from his lawyers. Chief of these in the early 1460s was Brian Roucliffe. Roucliffe's letters begin in 1461, addressing his employer simply, "Maister Sir William Plumpton, knight," as Roucliffe was sitting as third Baron of the Exchequer throughout this period.[62] "My advis being allwaies redy" Roucliffe insists, for his "especiall good maister," and he always signs his letters "your servant."[63] While a lawyer as well-placed as Roucliffe could do his master much good, the question of good mastership echoes throughout these letters, reminding us of the responsibilities that lords had to their men at every social level, and whatever economic or familial ties bound them together. Indeed, Roucliffe's position imposed limits on his usefulness to Plumpton at times. In Letter 2, Roucliffe reminds Plumpton that in a particular case, "I may nought be but of Counsell"; however, because of this hindrance, Roucliffe has "gotten that one [an attorney] shall appeare for you att the day of account." The letter dates to November 1461, when Plumpton was still in the Tower of London for his active Lancastrian sympathies. In 1463, another tie bound man and master: marriage, as Roucliffe's son contracted to marry Plumpton's granddaughter.[64] After this date, instead of signing himself Plumpton's "servant," Roucliffe identifies himself as a "serviceable brother."[65] In his final letter of this time period, he addresses Plumpton as his "intirly beloved brother, and singularly my good master."[66] Consider how this sobriquet recognizes Roucliffe's continuing usefulness to his employer, but simultaneously reminds Plumpton of their new tie.[67]

The correspondence of the Pastons, Stonors, and Plumptons help to flesh out the vocabulary introduced in chapter 1. Each of these letter writers was beholden to men above him in the social order, and held responsibilities to men below him as well. How these men handled negotiating these complex relationships could influence reputation, as it did for Stonor, or could impact a family's entire livelihood, as Plumpton's example clearly shows. When viewed from the level of the people involved in service, rather than from the vantage of estate records, it becomes clear that what defined "right" and "wrong" maintenance practices could be genuinely difficult to assess, even for the people involved. Service relationships could be used toward self-serving ends as well as serve as a positive means of community support. Chapter 3 will explore the service relationship that hit closest to home, that between a husband and a wife.

CHAPTER 3

ATTAINING WOMEN

A s we saw in chapter 1, medieval thinkers recognized a range of unequal relationships, such as lord and servant, abbot and monk, and husband and wife.[1] In each of these cases, a person made a decision to enter a relationship and legally relinquished his or her autonomy to another to greater or lesser degrees. Indeed, the use of these analogies in law and literature ought not surprise us, as Lynn Staley and other critics have noted that medieval authors, especially Chaucer, argue politically sensitive points by analogy.[2] In this chapter, we will concentrate on the relationship between wife and husband as an analogy for that between lord and retainer. Exploring the power dynamics between a lord and his retainer would have been potentially fraught for a medieval author, in part because the authors were usually of lesser status than the lords they described and critiqued. The analogous relationship between husbands and wives was ubiquitous, however, and utterly safe to criticize, as the authors benefited from their privileged position as men. These are all reasons that the married couple as a notion was "good to think with" for medieval English people.[3]

The constraints under which members of unequal relationships could find themselves recall Criseyde's "slydynge courage."[4] While the analogy is not perfect, we can recall how Criseyde in theory has perfect autonomy in her decision making: she is a widow, and can decide for herself. In practice, however, many influences constrain her decisions: to highlight a few, what information she does and does not receive from Pandarus, her actual ability to successfully escape the Greek camp, her own emotional world. The members of unequal relationships that I explore resemble the "diglossic" agents studied by Burger, who have responsibilities both above and below themselves in the social hierarchy.[5] In the following chapters I will borrow this notion of "slydynge courage" as "sliding" agency, or more carefully phrased, autonomy, a sliding agency experienced by diglossic men and women, skilled in the languages of agency and constraint.

Remember that premodern wives exhibited a state of sliding agency because they were in a legal state called coverture. They were *femme couverts* and legally the same person as their husbands, a legal fiction called "unity of person."[6] "Covered" by their husbands, wives in medieval Europe had no legal personhood or agency apart from their husbands. Technically, any civil activity the wife took part in that brought her into contact with the law brought her husband, rather than herself, into contact with the law. Now, obviously married women did have active lives in medieval England, participating in trade and acting locally as entrepreneurs, as well as more nefariously committing trespasses and felonies. Legal or illegal, they acted only with their husbands' blessings and in the pretense that they were legally *femmes soles*, or single women, uncovered by a husband. In a nutshell, a wife had autonomy that the law might or might not recognize, dependent on the circumstances and the willingness of her husband to cover her actions. Moreover, because wives were *couvert* but were capable of acting on their own initiative, they were dangerous in ways similar to retainers who could act on their own, and be protected by their lords.

In fact, parliament and the courts appear to be particularly anxious about the autonomy of women toward the end of the fourteenth century, the same time that these institutions legislate to control retinues.[7] Perhaps surprisingly, the legal example of this concern that I will trace in this chapter is the crime of rape.[8] Rape as we know it today is fairly easily defined in the law as forced coitus.[9] The medieval crime of *raptus*, however, could mean forced coitus, or it could mean abduction, or a combination of both. Whichever was implied, however, if a woman was legally her husband's person, then rape of a wife becomes a more complex crime than many critics have recognized.[10] In 1382, the first legislation against rape since the second Statute of Westminster (1285) was promulgated.[11] This so-called Statute of Rapes made significant strides to simultaneously recognize women's autonomy, and foreclose their opportunities to act in a legal capacity. While previously women could prosecute their own rapes by appealing their attackers as felons, now litigation had to be conducted by the nearest male relative. Moreover, whether or not a woman consented to her rape, she and her attacker were disinherited. A rape suit became, in short, a civil suit for damages incurred by the nearest male relative.[12] Since wives were incapable of making their own civil legal actions, technically, any action practiced on a wife transferred directly to the woman's husband. That rape legislation was tightened in the 1380s to ensure that it was solely an offense between men should lead us to reexamine literary depictions of rape cautiously to see whether they comment on this new development. As we shall see, depictions of rape in literature demonstrate anxiety about the autonomy of women similar to that expressed in the statute. Moreover, in literary narratives, men use women to test and renegotiate each others' power just as lords did with retainers. In short, we see the transitive property of married women used to attack men in literary examples of the rape of women.[13]

H. Marshall Leicester considers these issues from a deconstructionist perspective that provides useful for the inquiry in this chapter.[14] Leicester examines the distinction between statute law and the common law without recourse to legal history, and yet it is a distinction that critics using legal history, such as Christopher Cannon, demonstrate also.[15] Consider an extended example of the difference between statute and common law:

> Typically, statutes address a particular set of historical circumstances, and, in contrast to the give-and-take of cases, customary practices, precedents, and argument that makes common law a continually developing process, a statute attempts to *lay down the law* once and for all, and to settle the issue it addresses in a definitive way. A statute is the legal equivalent of reification: it tries to give

a determinate meaning to a state of affairs…and to specify procedures and penalties for ensuring that that meaning is sustained.[16]

Certainly this analogy describes the situations under examination
here: medieval marriage laws reified a particular arrangement of
power and autonomy.[17] Yet, actual marriages, and depictions of
marriage in texts, demonstrate, like common law, a far more complex power dynamic, resistant to codification in statutory form. I
believe that the questions Leicester asks about rape in the *Wife of
Bath's Tale* can stand for the historical position of rape in fourteenth-
century England more generally as well:

> To ask whether the punishment of death for rape is a matter of stat-
> ute or of common law is, as I have just suggested, to put in question
> the place of rape in relation to the normal course of events: is its
> place so firmly embedded in normal understanding that the crime
> and its punishment follow naturally from one another as cause and
> effect, or is the punishment for the crime (that is, the understanding
> of what sort of crime it is) sufficiently indeterminate to required
> a statutory interruption of the normal course, a special setting of
> penalties?[18]

As the repeated rape statutes demonstrate, while *a* definition of
rape was "embedded in normal understanding," a *legal* definition was not, but subject to debate and differentiation as culture
changed. Similarly, while maintenance was deeply understood by
all, its legal ramifications remained open to interpretation.

As nonintuitive as it might be, we hunt, then, for a way to examine service culture and maintenance through the dynamic nature
of late medieval attitudes toward rape. I can think of nowhere better to start than with Chaucer, the quintessential late-fourteenth-
century author who provides a range of depictions of rape in his
work.[19] There is no rape in the *Franklin's Tale*, yet the autonomy
of the wife, Dorigen, is the pivot around which the actions of the
men in the story turn, and the tale offers an excellent review of
how the coverture system worked. Similarly, the rape of Lucretia
in *Legend of Good Women* highlights how the raped wife's body
becomes the raped husband's body, and how this transitive action

moves the crime into a political arena. While Chaucer considers the most famous medieval rape story, that of Helen of Troy, surprisingly little in his works, I will take a moment and explore how this rape illustrates how the wide definition of rape, and the sliding autonomy of wives, leaves Helen's culpability in this case almost unknown. Despite this lack of knowledge, however, and in line with contemporary legislation, restitution is taken for Helen's ravishment. Lastly, in the *Wife of Bath's Tale* and one of its analogues, Chaucer provides an illustration of how the relationship between a husband and wife is analogous to that between a lord and his retainer.

The *Franklin's Tale* develops a situation in which a wife is at first allowed to retain her autonomy as a *femme sole,* but this situation appears to be impossible to maintain. While the knight Arveragus is on an extended sojourn in England to practice his chivalry, his noble wife Dorigen learns that a squire, Aurelius, loves her. Dorigen rejects him soundly, but adds jokingly that she will be his lover if he can remove all the rocks from the coastline of Brittany, and she swears an oath to this effect. A magician causes the rocks to disappear for Aurelius, in return for a thousand pound payment, so that after Arveragus returns home, Aurelius insists that Dorigen fulfill her oath. She laments, but tells Arveragus. Perhaps surprisingly he tells Dorigen "ye shul youre trouthe holden," but demands that she keep the liaison as secret as possible.[20] When Dorigen goes to meet Aurelius, she reveals that Arveragus has sent her, and Aurelius, shamed by the nobility of the gesture valuing a promise over his wife's chastity, releases Dorigen from her oath. Upon hearing the story, the magician releases Aurelius from his debt, and the Franklin asks which, the knight, the squire, or the clerk, was "mooste fre."[21]

   With the issue of autonomy so close to the surface of the *Franklin's Tale*, it is not surprising that a number of critics have explored various facets of the topic.[22] Susan Crane demonstrates how Dorigen's unstable position within the tale resembles franklins' unstable positions in the developing class structure of fourteenth-century

England. The analysis she draws between Dorigen's complex autonomy as a wife, and a group of men, like franklins, at the fringe of the service-system reminds us of the importance of examining marriage narratives with an eye toward larger power dynamics. Andrea Rossi-Reder argues that Chaucer's "expansion of women's roles lies not so much in a feminist consciousness, but in his interest in the differences between male and female agency."[23] Chaucer does precisely this, but Rossi-Reder misses the nuances of power resulting from the coverture system. Agency was not so simple as men being mobile and women being immobile. Corinne Saunders makes a very important connection when she identifies Dorigen's worst problem: "for Dorigen the gravest aspect of Aurelius' deception is not the threat of sexual shame *per se* but rather the power he wields over her by requiring her consent to adultery."[24] This statement gestures toward the no-win situation in which wives, or any person in an unequal relationship, could find themselves; without the autonomy to choose either yes or no, they faced the social expectation that they would say no, and yet were required to say yes.

Carolynn Van Dyke sees the issue of moral agency to be at the core of the *Franklin's Tale*, but like Rossi-Reder, does not take the full cultural context into account.[25] She argues that Chaucer persistently revises his source texts in order to develop moral agency for his female characters.[26] Van Dyke suggests that the goal of the *Franklin's Tale* is to claim "not simply that 'maistrie' should be shared in marriage, but that women are autonomous agents."[27] Van Dyke recognizes the equivocal nature of Dorigen's agency, and I would like to situate that troubled agency within the legalities of the medieval English marriage. Van Dyke states that "the same speech that spotlights Dorigen's ethical consciousness reveals equally clearly her impotence," and I contend that Chaucer is highlighting this impotence as one created by the coverture system.[28] Only its lack of cultural context leads me to disagree with Van Dyke's conclusion that Arveragus is iniquitous because "he is 'fre' with what no one can rightfully give, the ethical worth of another person."[29] From our modern perspective, I agree entirely with her. Yet the contemporary culture in which Chaucer wrote had constructed itself carefully so that Arveragus' autonomy is constrained in this matter as is Dorigen's; one can indeed have controlling influence over another's autonomy and not be malevolent in the fourteenth century. Chaucer and some of his contemporaries are beginning to question this state of affairs, but the process is yet too young to assume this iniquity of Arveragus.

Van Dyke's position agrees with Richard Firth Green's suggestion that English poets like Chaucer and Gower were concerned with moral and ethical double standards that applied differently to men and to women.[30] Moreover, Green demonstrates how the emphasis on keeping one's oath in the *Franklin's Tale* had legal resonance.[31] Green argues that Chaucer demonstrates "a far clearer recognition of the gap that was beginning to open up in the late fourteenth century between the morality and the law of promise-keeping" than most other authors of the day and had an understanding of the complexities of Ricardian law.[32] In the spirit of Green, I want to push Van Dyke's conception of the level of these authors' enculturation a step further and engage the social and legal power dynamics surrounding marriage.

Drawing from Elizabeth Fowler's work, Francine McGregor examines the *Franklin's Tale* with consideration for Dorigen's legal standing in coverture.[33] McGregor's consideration of coverture has a number of important repercussions for readings of the tale: "the narrative confers on [Dorigen] a mode of agency she has abdicated (it asserts that her oath to Aurelius is literal and binding), simultaneously appropriates that agency as Arveragus's (he insists that she fulfill her oath), and goes on to explore the interaction between the two men."[34] McGregor recognizes that the *Franklin's Tale* is an effort to illustrate the fictional civil death of the wife becoming reality. She notes that Arveragus' honor is threatened if Dorigen fails to keep her word to Aurelius, and that "Arveragus manag[ing] to figure his will as hers" is precisely the state of affairs under coverture.[35] In this interpretation, Dorigen is aware of the patriarchal structures she inhabits and is wary of Arveragus' offer of freedom. Moreover, McGregor realizes that the unequal relationship

between a husband and wife opens up a two-way street: "her relin-
quishing of sovereignty to Arveragus provides her with a means
of resisting other social demands."[36] Indeed, I would argue that
by allowing Arveragus to constrain her autonomy, Dorigen gains
certain claims on Arveragus' own autonomy. McGregor's appli-
cation of Fowler's arguments to the *Franklin's Tale* was a necessary
addition to the critical reception of this tale. I want to talk through
a similar interpretation of the *Franklin's Tale*, and demonstrate step
by step how coverture influences agencies of all sorts throughout the tale. Thus, an analysis of the *Franklin's Tale* can serve as an
introduction that sets the themes of this chapter into their wider
cultural context.

Dorigen's autonomy is insisted upon throughout the first sections of the story. When he asks for Dorigen's hand in marriage,
Arveragus, "of his free wyl he swoor hire as a knyght, / That nevere
in al his lyf he.../ Ne sholde upon hym take no maistrie / Agayn
hir wyl," but only "the name of soveraynetee, / That wolde he have
for shame of his degree."[37] Dorigen's power of self-determination
seems assured in this relationship. In legal terms, although she will
be *femme couvert* in name, Arveragus swears that she will in fact be
femme sole. Moreover, once Arveragus leaves for England, Dorigen is
in precisely the position that gave medieval noblewomen their greatest freedom of all; they ran the estate in their husbands' absence.[38]

In fact, Dorigen's autonomy is the basis on which the problem of the tale rests. When Dorigen makes her fateful promise:
"whan ye han maad the coost so clen / Of rokkes that ther nys
no stoon ysene, / Thanne wol I love yow best of any man," she is
acting as a *femme sole*, for Arveragus is still in England.[39] However,
when Aurelius performs this trick, Arveragus has returned from
England, and so Dorigen is *femme couvert*, publicly, at least. In light
of the invisible rocks, Dorigen considers privately the conditions
surrounding her promise as though she could be forced to fulfill the articles of it legitimately: "she wende nevere han come in
swich a trappe. /.../ 'For wende I nevere by possibilitee / That
swich a monstre or merveille myghte be! / It is agayns the proces
of nature.' "[40] Wives could not make legal promises without the

permission of their husbands under the system of coverture, but Dorigen here reacts as though her promise is a good one, regardless of what Arveragus might say about it.

The next section of the text demonstrates Dorigen's capacity to consider independent action. Arveragus has briefly left town, so technically, Dorigen is once again *femme sole* in the eyes of the law.[41] She must "know [her] fals, or lese [her] name," she claims, and can find only one route out of her predicament: death.[42] To support her decision, Dorigen embarks on a long lament to virgins and wives who have chosen death rather than submit to rape.[43] In doing so, Dorigen highlights the autonomy of these women: while suicide is a final act (perhaps *the* final act), these women are making this decision on their own, for their own persons. Moreover, this lament functions as an internal debate. Dorigen claims that "I wol conclude that it is bet for me / To sleen myself than been defouled thus."[44] It is better for *herself*, and is an action of her own will supported by due examination of Biblical and classical examples of women faced with related circumstances.

Nevertheless, most of the women in Dorigen's lament have lost their father or their husband; they are *femmes soles* out of necessity, and are relatively free to act on their own initiatives in a way we cannot be sure Dorigen is. Dorigen has a husband, who returns home a few days after Aurelius' demand. When Dorigen shares her secret with Arveragus, the audience is reminded of his promise when they married, that he would only have the "soveraynetee" in public, and that she should make her own decisions in private. This moment appears to be a defining one in identifying how much autonomy Dorigen really has.[45]

In the end, it appears that Dorigen experiences the same sliding agency characteristic of all wives and retainers in England. We are not told whether Dorigen asks for Arveragus' input or not, simply that she tells him her tale. We are given Arveragus' response, which is supposed to surprise us: "ye shul youre trouthe holden, by my fay!"[46] Given Dorigen's thoughts concerning suicide, we are lead to hope that Arveragus steps in and asserts his legal authority to render Dorigen's promise void by disapproving of it, even though this would contradict his own promise to her in the beginning of the tale. Instead, Arveragus follows through and demands that Dorigen make good on her oath as any man would: "trouthe is the hyeste thyng that *man* may kepe."[47] Of course, because of the power dynamic between a husband and a wife under coverture, in the act of demanding that Dorigen show the autonomy of a man, he denies her that very independence. (Although as we shall see later, Dorigen *does* show the autonomy of a man: a *retainer.*) The relationship between this husband and wife parallels the fluidity Leicester sees in the common law until Arveragus steps in to clarify the situation, and *lay down the law* in his marriage, in an attempt to define, to fix, the degree of her autonomy relative to his, just as a statute would have.

The moment that Dorigen's agency is firmly fixed as that of a *femme couvert*, the tale turns into a competition between a series of men. In attempting to gain control over Dorigen, Aurelius is simultaneously making an implicit power play against Arveragus. The response we expect from Arveragus, to deny Dorigen's oath, would reinforce his coverture of her and serve as a flat denial that Aurelius has any power over him. Nevertheless, Arveragus' complex response highlights his power as lord of his wife. Dorigen's oath will stand, Arveragus insists, as he has promised to uphold her autonomy; however, it does not matter, as Arveragus has already demonstrated his control over Dorigen. There is no room for Aurelius in this picture, a point he realizes when Dorigen communicates to him her husband's will.

Moreover, Arveragus granting Dorigen's promise validity opens the door to the magician letting Aurelius out of his contract. Unlike Dorigen, Aurelius' ability to make a contract is not in question. However, as we have seen, depending on the perspective Dorigen is either able or unable to seal a contract. When Arveragus grants her contract validity, Aurelius finds himself unable to keep his side of the agreement without shame, and he does not carry through the agreement: "thus kan a squier doon a gentil dede / As wel as kan a knyght, withouten drede."[48] The magician lets Aurelius out of his payment contract for a similar reason.

As in the Statute of Rapes, Dorigen's consent hardly matters in this extended discussion of what is, from a modern perspective, a potential rape. Aurelius chooses not to force Dorigen to fulfill her ill-considered promise, but had he, the text (and Arveragus) insists that Dorigen would have been forced into sex she did not choose. Both oaths are related in a sort of agency-equation: in insisting that Dorigen uphold her oath, Arveragus upholds his promise to leave Dorigen her own agent at the same time as he denies her the autonomy to do so. His insistence leaves Arveragus himself open to a kind of assault, and demonstrates the dangers of the legal union of person. We will see how this transitive property between a husband and wife can have political repercussions next, in the Lucretia story.

The various versions of the Lucretia story explore directly how the sliding agency of wives was integrated into the power dynamics of the male political world. The story demonstrates the events that force a *laying down of the law*, in Leicester's words, in an effort to reify power hierarchies whose fluidity has become threatening. In outline, the story is simple. Tarquin, a prince of the Roman royal house, and one of his generals, Collatine, hold a contest about whose wife is best while they are out laying siege to a town. The pair leave the siege, sneak into Collatine's house, and spy on his wife, Lucretia, who is working with wool and bemoaning Collatine's absence. Tarquin is incited to lust at this unforced display of domesticity, returns the next evening, and rapes Lucretia at sword-point. The next day she calls her father and Collatine to her and recounts her rape. Despite her father's and husband's assurances that she is blameless, she kills herself. All authors cite the rape as the reason for the fall of the Tarquins and the end of Roman monarchy.

Most critical consideration of the legend of Lucretia concentrates on single versions, and while this has resulted in an array of interesting and important readings, a range of popular versions deserves to be considered within their cultural context.[49] While looking at single versions allows us to concentrate on one author's reading of a text, often in the context of the larger work in which the story is found, I am fascinated by how prevalent the story itself was. Only by examining several versions of the Lucretia story can we begin to discuss the cultural work the tale accomplishes. At the same time, my interest is in the Lucretia story itself, so I am less interested here than some critics in the role that her tale plays in the larger works into which it is set. So for example, Craig Bertholet writes insightfully about Gower's version of the Lucretia tale in the *Confessio Amantis*, and declares that it alone of the popular medieval retellings examines the story from a sociopolitical context.[50] Yet, I argue that when viewed within the context of the literature of late medieval England, any text about rape had a sociopolitical context, and that other authors, like Chaucer and Lydgate, were as aware of this fact as Gower. Perhaps the most complex version of the tale is delivered by Lydgate, who is almost entirely absent from the criticism.[51]

The narrative structure of the story aided Middle English authors in concentrating on a few moments where agency is highlighted: the rape itself, where Tarquin asks Lucretia to choose to be raped, the moment in which Lucretia refuses the pity of her family in favor of suicide, and the decision the family makes to overthrow the Tarquins. The manner in which each author deals with these scenes enables us to explore the understanding of power relations, like marriage and maintenance that simultaneously protected and illustrated problems with unequal relationships.

As in the *Franklin's Tale* Lucretia participates in the sliding agency of a wife or retainer. When her husband is away at war, she must act as *femme sole*, keeping up the household in his absence. Indeed, in all versions, Lucretia's dedicated domesticity is part of her attraction for Tarquin. The rape itself is a moment of deepest irony. Lucretia is literally a covered woman when Tarquin abducts Collatine's place in the conjugal bed, and then Tarquin demands that she make a decision about whether to struggle and die in infamy or submit to rape as if she were *femme sole* and had the autonomy to choose (or deny) a sexual partner for herself. Lucretia experiences aporia when faced with this cascade of problematic decisions, at once practical, ethical, and legal, and she loses consciousness. On coming to, Lucretia's first act is to call her friends to her, and she continues to act for herself; denying her family's insistence that since she was not at fault Collatine's name would not suffer, she stabs herself.

Each author presents Lucretia with a slightly different choice during the rape scene. Chaucer's Tarquin emphasizes the impotence of Lucretia's agency. "Maugre hyre, she shal my leman be!" declares Tarquin, echoing Chaucer's phrasing in the *Wife of Bath's Tale* when the maiden is raped "maugree hir heed."[52] Tarquin's criminality is highlighted further as "in the nyght ful thefly gan he stalke."[53] Gower ups the ante and calls Tarquin a tyrant and a traitor. Like Chaucer's, Gower's Tarquin admits that he will have Lucretia "althogh it were ayein hire wille," granting her agency to refuse, but be denied that refusal.[54] Both Chaucer's and Lydgate's Tarquin demand that Lucretia choose between rape and murder as an apparent adulteress.[55] If Chaucer's Lucretia began the "crye or noyse" required by law to identify a rape, Tarquin would kill her and a place a dead stable boy in her bed, claiming that he had killed both after finding them in adultery.[56] Gower's Lucretia faces a different choice than Chaucer's or Lydgate's: however, for here Tarquin promises to kill her "and hire folk aboute" if she tries to raise an alarm.[57] Apparent adultery is not the additional threat here, but that of being a poor proxy for her husband, being a poor *femme sole*, and causing household members to be killed. In the *Legend of Good Women* and the *Confessio Amantis*, Lucretia never makes a decision, passing out "for fer of sclaunder and drede of deth" since in no case could she be a good *femme couvert*.[58]

Lydgate points the problem of the complex agency of wives even further: "but she wolde assent" to her own rape Tarquin would murder her and a boy as apparent adulterers.[59] In Lydgate particularly we are confronted with a rape that even modern American courts would recognize with difficulty, for constrained or not, in *Fall of Princes*, Lucretia consents. Lydgate's text reminds us that the medieval laws made the victim's consent irrelevant, and puts pressure on this fact: here a woman's "assent" is clearly not consent.[60] As Ireland reminds us, "recall that in English law the offense of rape is an offense not simply against women . . . After the 1382 statute...Lucrece is an accomplice, albeit an unwilling one, in the crime against her husband."[61]

Across the board, despite her husband's desire that she live and thrive, Lucretia exercises the personal agency of a *femme sole* in choosing suicide over living dishonor. In Elizabeth Robertson's words, Lucretia is free to act because "just after rape, a woman's subjectivity is released from the social constraints that determine not only her value or worth as property, but also her identity."[62] However, as we have already seen, all wives experienced such sliding agencies throughout their lives. Chaucer's Lucretia refuses the forgiveness of her "hire frendes alle, / fader, moder, husbonde all yfeere" in favor of suicide to save her husband's honor.[63] The open, public declarations of Chaucer's Lucretia contrast with the literally closed-door admissions of Gower's character: Lucretia's father, Collatine, and cousin Brutus wait for privacy: "the chambre Dore anon was stoke, / Er thei have oght unto hire spoke."[64] Gower's Lucretia's reason for suicide is more independent than Chaucer's character as well, for this Lucretia dies to protect *her* name, not her husband's.[65] At first glance, Lydgate's character appears to be the most independent of all: "the morwen afftir she list nothyng concele, / Tolde hir husbonde hooli the gouernaunce, / *Hym requeryng* for to do vengaunce / Vpon this crym."[66] While Chaucer's and Gower's characters act as if the unity between husband and wife is broken after the rape, as if both Lucretias were again *femme sole*, Lydgate's character recognizes her rights within coverture. Telling Collatine everything, she *demands* that he defend her honor by pursuing vengeance. Wives and retainers were not the only ones whose autonomy could be constrained: lords could also be subject to demands upon which they would have to act, as we recall of Thomas Stonor in chapter 2.

In Gower, Lucretia's moment of complete lack of agency, her loss of consciousness, is paralleled in a similar moment experienced by her husband and father. Because she is already dead civilly, Lucretia's physical death in the face of her family's denial of her desire to die causes them aporia similar to that Lucretia faced during her rape: "hire housebonde, hire fader eke / Aswoune upon the bodi felle" in a tragic final act of coverture.[67] It is left to Brutus to take action for the family: he leaps to Lucretia's side, removes the sword from her body, and swears vengeance. Lucretia's final conscious thoughts are on Brutus, as "sche tho made a contienance, / Hire dedlich yhe and ate laste / In thonkinge as it were up caste."[68] While her father and husband are covering her body with theirs as she lays dying, it is Brutus who will "cover" her intention and instigate her revenge.

The manner in which each author describes the events leading up to the fall of the Tarquins helps to articulate precisely the connection each sees between personal agency and the larger political structure. Chaucer begins and ends his versions of the Lucretia story by gesturing toward the ultimate result of her rape: the downfall of the Tarquins and end of the Roman monarchy.[69] Following her briefly narrated suicide, Chaucer goes on at some length to describe Brutus' oath of vengeance against the Tarquins, and "ne never was ther kyng in Rome toun / Syn thilke day."[70] The connection between Lucretia's action and the fall of the Tarquins is direct in Lydgate: "and bi occasioun off this pitous deede, / Tarquyn exilid, and hooli his kenreede, / For whiche cause, be record off writyng, / Was ther neuer in Rome the cite, / Afftir that day no man crownyd kyng."[71] Recall that because of her civil death, a wife's legal action could only be considered valid if affirmed by her husband. Lucretia's physical death punctuates this legal truism ironically, as it forces her family to recognize her autonomy, and as good lords and husbands, seek redress after the fact. Through the transitive property of service relations, the attack on Collatine's wife became an attack on the entire family and results in a total disintegration of the political structure.

Lydgate explores the complex relationship between the agencies of husbands and wives most thoroughly in Lucretia's long complaint in Book III of the *Fall of Princes*. His previous discussion of Lucretia occurred in Book II, and was based on a historical source, but the ultimate source for the Book III lament is Ovid. Rather than a narration, or set of dialogues between Lucretia and her husband, this lament emphasizes Lucretia's emotional response to her rape. While the emotional impact of this version is readily acknowledged, few critics have noted that Lydgate's translation of this passage is designed with legal process in mind. Although Lydgate translates quite closely from his French source, Laurent de Premierfait here, so the text is not based on the common law at this point, Lucretia's *planctus* would have been recognizable still as a legal maneuver to Lydgate's audience. Lydgate's Lucretia is intimately aware of the law that binds herself to her husband and how Tarquin's crime acts against that bond, and against Collatine himself.

Lucretia employs the fiction that she is presenting a case in court, the court of her husband; her lament resembles more a legal complaint than a literary one. Moreover, she sets up the fiction that she is giving testimony in a court of civil law, or "equite." As we saw earlier, medieval analogies ran thusly: a wife is to a husband, a subject is to his lord, and therefore as subject and wife Lucretia applies to her lord-husband's court of law for redress.[72] She reminds Collatine that as "lord and husbonde" his duty is "[her] bodi to gouerne," and we ought to remember that to usurp a lord's place over his subjects is treason.[73] Only after this level of court hears the plea may the case be moved to a higher court with the power to effect change.

Lucretia leans upon the legal unity of person experienced by husband and wife to make her case against Tarquin. She begins by emphasizing the legal bond uniting herself and Collatine into a single, legal entity: "as I Lucrece / Am be the lawe ioyned in mariage / To the, my lord."[74] "I will no mor no quarell take on honde / Nor in no wise make non accioun, / Withoute that thou list," Lucretia says, and her words remind us of the legal constraints facing a raped woman.[75] Technically, following the Statute of Rapes, Lucretia cannot take up her quarrel in court, or even present an action for trespass: indeed after 1382, only after her husband heard her story might he choose to pursue legal redress for damages. Here Lucretia recognizes her civil death and also acknowledges the reality of the courts. However as Kelly and Cannon remind us, despite the statute law, rapes did continue to be appealed.[76] Even so, Lucretia chooses civil death: she "will not" appeal her rape herself.

Lucretia's civil death is not a passive one, however, as she makes clear in the rest of the complaint. She next identifies the reciprocity inherent in the union of persons: "iniurie doon or any maner wrong / ageyn my worshepe or myn honeste, / Bi the lawe my sentence is maad strong, / It touchet[h] you also weel as me, / I am so hooli yolden onto the."[77] A legal wrong done to Lucretia is a legal wrong done to Collatine: it touches them both. At the same time, however, this passage highlights Lucretia's strength within the marriage as her own person. Her speech is "sentence," and her use of "yolden" suggests knightly surrender to a better knight, an action that, while subordinate, was hardly ignominious.[78] Knightly surrender also serves as a metaphoric reminder of the duties the victorious knight had toward the vanquished. Here Lucretia is demanding rights accruing to her as the subordinate party in an unequal agency relationship. Moreover, Lydgate emphasizes the union of persons several more times in the following stanzas.[79]

Although they are one person legally, Lucretia recognizes their physical separation at the same time. They share "o will" but she uses this fact to introduce the notion that "I mut disclose to you the gret outrage / Doon onto *me*."[80] The legal fiction of unity of person has been uncovered in Lucretia's raped body. Now, the best she can do to reinstate the fiction is to tell her husband of the event, and apprise him that he was raped by proxy, through his wife: "reherse I will, so that ye sauff it vouche, / A mortall wrong which the & me doth touche."[81] She must convey to him that a crime that has been committed against him, so that he may move against Tarquin, *Collatine's* attacker.

The beginning of Lucretia's narration of the facts of the case illustrates the similarity between duties of the wife to a husband and duties of a retainer to a lord. Consider the following stanza:

> In a castell which callid is Collace,
> Off which my lord heer hath the gouernaunce,
> Tarquyn the yonge cam into that place.
> I, full diswarre to make purueiaunce
> Ageyn his comyng or any ordenaunce,
> Toforn nat warnyd off his officeris,
> Sat onpurueied among my chaumbereris.[82]

Certainly the topic is one of domestic administration and lack of preparation to welcome an honored guest. However, the vocabulary ("place," "purueiaunce," "ordenaunce") works equally well as an analogy to Lucretia's military defense of a castle, one of the jobs noble wives were occasionally called upon to perform, and a regular duty of affines. As I have mentioned before, it also highlights that, although still a wife, as commander of a castle, Lucretia is as much a *femme sole* as a *femme couvert* the night that Tarquin arrives.[83]

Lydgate's Lucretia prefaces her account of the act by pointing out that Tarquin was in contravention of two legal systems, the civil and the natural, "in my persone offendyng bothe too."[84] Of course, Tarquin offends the English common law as well, but in each case, Lucretia identifies her own body as the site of offense, even while narrating the event to her husband as one that affects him as well. The wrongs Lucretia recounts are two, one against Collatine's house, and one against Collatine's wife's body. Tarquin "be his fals[e] subtil compassyng / He gan espie thestris off the place," in an expansion of the legal phrase *ex malicia precogitata* (with malice aforethought) so often invoked in common law felony suits, and then proceeds to attack Lucretia.[85]

Lucretia must emphasize Tarquin's ill intent in her testimony because this is not a case of housebreaking; Tarquin was invited in with as much ceremony as Lucretia could muster, given the lack of notice. "His ent[e]ryng was meek and debonaire," she recalls, "his cheer contrarie onto his corage."[86] Given his status, Lucretia "roos up meekli and gan hym to salue, / As appertened in alle maner thynge / Onto the sone off a worthi kyng."[87] Technically, this case could not be argued this way in common law court in Lydgate's England; only in civil, "prerogative" courts like the Court of Chancery could intent be an official consideration.[88] Certainly, in presenting her case to her husband, Lucretia is in a kind of prerogative court, as future legal action is solely based on Collatine's decision. The Court of Chancery, in fact, was known unofficially as the Court of Conscience or Court of Equity soon after its inception; that Lucretia goes to her husband looking for equity is particularly poignant here. Indeed, it is possible that the common law's lack of interest in intent assisted in its (to modern eyes) odd, multiform definition of rape. In the common law, women could not have intent (to be raped, or not to be raped), but neither could men. As would have the common law, criticism has failed to take into account Tarquin's intent, despite the fact that it was critical to legal understanding of the civil crime in this story.

In the end, this attack opens a dangerous fissure in Lucretia and Collatine's unity of person, and only Collatine has the power to acknowledge the breach as permanent or to believe in Lucretia's victimization, to accept himself as a ravished party, and to seek redress. "Mi spousaile broke," Lucretia laments, and declares that "I am nat worthi that men me sholde call, / . . . / . . . / . . . / Off Collatyn from hen[ne]sfoorth the wiff."[89] She appears to fear that she is again *femme sole* without the protection of coverture. She sees two options for Collatine: to condemn her or to revenge her. Only Collatine has the quasi-judicial power to break the unity of person permanently or to remake it: "yiff if seeme in your opynyoun, / In this caas I sholde been onpure, / I will receyue iust punycioun," otherwise "lat myn Iniurie and this mortal cryme / Be [. . .] pun[y]shed off riht and equite, / Withoute delay."[90] Lucretia invokes "right and equity," a formula often found in pleas before Chancery, and after deliberation Chancery decisions were swift and final. As if judges in Chancery, Collatine and Lucretia's father, who is also hearing this narration, take all due deliberation before coming to a decision: "thei longe hadde musid / On this compleynt in ther inward siht."[91] They decide to fully excuse Lucretia from any wrong and to choose vengeance on Tarquin.

The popularity of the Lucretia story suggests contemporary interest in inequality between husbands and wives and illustrates how those relationships could be targets between men in struggles for political power. The Lucretia stories are usually approached as histories, or at least *exempla*, model stories demonstrating important morals and ethics. The Trojan war stories balance between the genres of history and *romance* to explore similar issues. Perhaps because of its frequent reception as history, the most famous rape in medieval literature, that of Helen of Troy, receives relatively little consideration in the texts that pivot around her *raptus*. Nevertheless, Colin Fewer claims that the characters of Lydgate's version of the story display a "superabundance of agency."[92] This is an important lens through which to view medieval opinions of Helen, and implicitly, of rape, in each of the texts surveyed here. Helen was a wife, and therefore should have demonstrated the sliding agency that we find characteristic of wives. However, as we examine the texts, it is clear that Helen's agency slides more than it "should," or, perhaps more conservatively, the narrative points to the dangers of the ability of wives' agencies to slide. Therefore, Helen provides an interesting case to consider when examining the move in later medieval England to deemphasize a woman's consent to her sexual "attack"; as Saunders puts it, "the medieval metamorphoses of Helen articulate contemporary uncertainty regarding consent."[93]

I am basing my comments on Lydgate's *Troy Book* as the most influential single Middle English version of the story.[94] Lydgate's translation, together with Guido delle Colonne's Latin original provide the versions of the Troy story that are used right through Marlowe and Sidney.[95] For a slightly earlier comparison, I will include contrasting discussion from the short *raptus*-narrative in Gower's *Confessio Amantis*, and the Laud Troy Book, another Middle English version of Guido's text dating to about 1400.[96] In no instance is Helen's rape more than an occasional touchstone in the narratives.[97]

The outline of the Helen story hardly needs to be summarized, as her abduction from Menelaus by Paris of Troy, instigating the Trojan War, is infamous. However, less well known to the generalist, is that this famous *raptus* of a wife is preceded by a lesser-known one of a spinster in both shorter and long versions of the Troy story. A generation earlier, the old city of Troy is attacked by the Greeks and Priam's sister Hesione is captured and given to Telamon as spoils of war. Once Priam rebuilds Troy, he hopes to regain Hesione as a goodwill gesture to avoid further war. The Greeks refuse the Trojan overtures, and the ground is set for Paris' raid in which he captures Helen.

Even Gower's short text includes mention of Hesione, the earlier victim of *raptus*, and links one *raptus* to the next. When the Greeks burn Troy, they take many prisoners, "among whiche ther was on, / The kinges doughter Lamedon, / Esiona, that faire thing, / Which unto Thelamon the king / Be Hercules and be thassent / Of al the hole parlement / Was at his wille yove and granted."[98] Gower's insistence that Hesione was handed over by unanimous assent of parliament highlights the collective decision involved in this *raptus*. As much as Hesione is raped by an individual, she is also raped by an entire country. Similarly, after Hector is snubbed by the Greeks in his request for Hesione's return, the Trojan parliament debates seriously before agreeing to send Paris to Greece.[99] These rapes are depicted as actions between men, and the women's links to specific men makes them targets of entire nations.

The more full renditions of Guido's narrative go into detail about Hesione's *raptus* and agree that the slight is not simply in the abduction, but also in the disrespectful manner of her keeping. Lydgate comes down strongly against the poor fashion of Hesione's capture: "For syth he gat hir þat day be victorie, / For his worschip and his owne glorie, / Havyng rewarde to hir hige degre, / He schulde rather of kyngly honeste, / And of knygthood, haue weddid hir þerfore, / Syth þat sche was of blood so gentil bore, / Þan of fals lust, ageyn al godlyhede, / Vsed hir bewte and hir womanhede / Dishonestly, and in synful wyse."[100] Having abducted Hesione, Telamon does not treat her as the sister of a king and marry her, and this class-based slight is as great as the abduction and rape itself to Lydgate. The Laud Troy Book emphasizes Hesione's *raptus* as the impetus for the Trojan War, marginalizing Helen in the process: "so weylaway! That sche was born! / Se fele gode men for here were lorn / Afftirward wel many a day, / .... / For bi here roos al the wo, / That sixti thousand knygtes and mo / Deyed for her, and al her kyn," and "For hir rape the deth ther fonged."[101] Laud also recognizes that Telamon does ill by not marrying Hesione and repeatedly refers to Hesione being kept in "hordome."[102]

Since Hesione is unmarried, her *raptus* reflects the lack of permission of her nearest male kin, Priam, and as typical of virgin abductions in the Middle Ages, efforts are made to effect the marriage of the two parties.[103] (Unlike Helen's *raptus*, we get no narration of Hesione's ideas about the matter.) Yet, Telamon refuses adamantly to do so, in a way perpetuating the state of *raptus*. With no marriage or return home to fix Hesione's agency onto a man in a formal way, her *raptus* continues for years. Telamon's refusal to marry Hesione, to unify their persons, or to return her to her brother's protection and agency reinforces the political nature of the possession: in prolonging Hesione's state of *raptus*, Greece continues to disparage Troy. Yet, Christopher Cannon points out common law's disinterest in consent before *or* after the fact, and notes that Paris and Helen *did* marry.[104] Indeed, the difference in treatment of Helen's and Hesione's rapes in literature locates the dichotomy between legal agency, and the very real autonomy that medieval men recognized that women exercised.

Hesione's theft as obvious spoils of war gives her *raptus* a clarity of interpretation that we cannot have for Helen, as a wife enabled with sliding agency. Gower mentions that Helen was attracted to Paris, but fails to identify whether or not she consented to her *raptus*.[105] Both Lydgate and the Laud-poet recount in detail Helen's agreement and assistance in her abduction. Not only does Lydgate point out that Helen was attracted to Paris, "þe fresche quene Eleyne / As hote brent in herte pryuely, / . . . . / For sche þougt sche had neuer aforn, / Of alle men þat euer yet wer born / Sey non so fair," but they "her hertise conceit declare secrely" to the effect that "concluded han, with schort avisement, / Fully þe fyn of her boþe entent, / And sette a purpose atwix hem in certeyn, / Whan þei cast for to mete ageyn."[106] If there is any doubt left as to Helen's willing participation in the abduction, during the event itself, Lydgate points out that Paris "hir enbrasiþ in his armys tweyn, / Ful humblely & with gret reuerence, / In whom he fonde no maner resistence; / . . . / For to Paris sche yalde hir outterly; / Hir hert in hap was yolde or sche cam þere, / Þerfor to yelde hir sche had lasse fere; / Sche can nat stryve, nor no woman scholde."[107] The Laud-poet similarly notices Helen and Paris' mutual attraction, and states clearly that "sche wolde wel fayn haue ben his wyue" and that after a discussion, they "were bothe at one assente."[108]

As statute law and the cases of Dorigen and Lucretia demonstrate, however, what exactly Helen's consent to her abduction means is less than clear. Lydgate's character Achilles suggests at one point that Helen's adultery frees Menelaus to marry again.[109] Both Lydgate and the Laud-poet point out that once onboard ship, Helen has second thoughts about her decision. These thoughts reinforce the existence of her own autonomy, and further confuse the question of whether she was considered to have the ability to consent to the abduction or not. In Lydgate, Helen "gan ful rewfully compleyne / Hir vnkouþe lyf, to dwelle with straungers, / ... / Fer sequestrid a-weye from hir contre, / Solitarie in captiuite," and specifically mourns "þat sche so fer aw-way / Departid is from hir Menelaus."[110] When Paris insists that she will live in more honor and luxury in Troy than in Greece, Helen points out that "wher me be loth or lef, / Sith I am kaugt & take at þis meschef, / Vn-to your wil I may nat now with-seie; / I am so bounde, þat I most obeie."[111] In fact, Helen finally determines that she must accept the fact of the *raptus* "sith goddis han as now ordeyned" the act and "maugre my wil, of necessite, / Fully to obeye what [Paris wants] to do with me."[112] In the end, it is difficult to determine how much autonomy Helen had when she initially made plans with Paris, and how much the decision of the gods is given as an excuse.

Yet, Fewer's contention that Helen's agency is "superabundant" seems to hold true, at least at first glance. Initially, at least, Helen appears to be "her own" woman, happily plotting an infidelity with Paris as her husband would not have had her do. Yet the signs get cloudy as we approach the *raptus* itself; as in law, a woman's consent had ceased to matter in defining a rape. Helen's consent is impossible to determine, despite her perhaps superabundant agency. Once in Troy, Helen marries Paris, an action that would fix her excessive agency with Paris', theoretically. Moreover, because of Helen's legal unity with her first husband, the king of Sparta, Paris' marriage to Helen can be seen as a symbolic attempt at control over Sparta, just as Hesione's perpetuated *raptus* is a lever against Troy. As with

Lucretia, Helen's civil *raptus* highlights the distance between wives' autonomy and civil death, and illustrates how unequal relationships could be manipulated for political ends. The *Wife of Bath's Tale* continues to consider women's autonomy in comparison to mens', but does so within the frame of a radically different genre, *romance*. Given the tale's analogues, the story of "what women most want" engages implicitly not just inequality between husbands and wives, but also between lords and their noble servants.

Chaucer's Wife of Bath needs no introduction; however, her short tale has received less critical attention than her long prologue. Beginning with a rape, the *Wife of Bath's Tale* links the issues of sexual and legal autonomy, and a close analogue, the *Weddynge of Sir Gawain and Dame Ragnell* further connects the issue of autonomy with lord and retainer relationships. In the *Wife of Bath's Tale*, we see how a story of forced coitus is used conversely to highlight the power of women inside union of person relationships. While the wife's autonomy changes most in a marriage, the husband's, too, is constrained in ways it had not been before the union. Similarly, both lord and retainer experience analogous constraint as seen in the mutual obligations between Gawain and Arthur in the *Weddynge of Sir Gawain and Dame Ragnell*.

In the *Wife of Bath's Tale*, the rape begins the action of the narrative swiftly, and is superseded just as swiftly by the question-quest. A nameless knight rapes a nameless maiden while riding along one day. The case goes to court and Arthur sentences the knight to death according to due process and the law. Guinevere begs that the knight's sentencing be moved into her power, however, and her court of ladies revise Arthur's death penalty in favor of rehabilitative justice: the knight is given a year and a day to discover the answer to the question of what women most want. The knight travels the country, but there seems to be no single answer to the question. As the term of the stay-of-execution nears its end, the knight finds an old woman who claims to be able to tell him the answer in return for his oath that he will grant her wish if her answer is correct. The knight sees no better option, and agrees, swearing the oath. Once again at Guinevere's court of ladies, the knight suggests that "sovereynetee" is what women most want, and the court grants him his life. The old woman demands her boon: to be married to the knight. Constrained, the knight agrees, but has difficulty on the wedding night consummating the marriage. After a pillow lecture in which the old woman argues that nobility resides in deeds, not genealogy or looks, the old woman gives the knight another choice: she will remain old and ugly, and be faithful, or she can be young, beautiful, and her husband will have to "take [his] aventure of the repair."[113] Cornered once again, the knight turns the decision over to his new wife, whereupon the old woman declares him to have given the correct response, to have given her sovereignty, and she declares that she will be beautiful and true to him.

Critical examination of the Wife of Bath is a scholarly industry unto itself, and so it is no surprise that there is a body of criticism that considers the roles of the law and subjectivity in relation to the tale. Critics such as Gerald Richman note how the tale highlights the two-way nature of the marriage debt; both husband and wife have claims on each other.[114] Richman does not, however, compare the marriage debt, a religious institution with the legal practice of unity of person. Robert Blanch demonstrates how gender and law twine together throughout the tale in "a fragmented social structure in which women illegitimately employ the coercive power of law in order to reinforce the concept of female sovereignty."[115] Blanch notes how Guinevere co-opts due process in an effort to gain power over men and still retain an illusion of hierarchical authority. I agree with Blanch that the female co-optation of a traditionally male legal system highlights problems with that system; however, I believe that gender and the law in the tale demonstrate problems with unequal relationships that could be figured by pairs of men and women, but could also be figured by pairs of men, as we shall see in the *Weddynge of Sir Gawain and Dame Ragnell*.

As has been mentioned before, Chaucer's description of the rape itself is a tour de force of compressed narrative.[116] The virgin is raped, "maugree hir heed, / By verray force," both legal phrases that establish the virgin's lack of consent and the felonious

forcefulness that the knight employed in his attack.[117] The hue
and cry, or "clamor" was raised and the community brought the
case before the highest judge in the land: the king.[118] Due process,
"cours of lawe" is followed, and the rapist is sentenced to death,
"swich was the statut."[119] In this way the rape is recognized, but in
under ten lines, and this is the last the audience hears of it.

Lack of autonomy is highlighted again only once the so-called
Loathly Lady demands that the knight fulfill his oath and marry
her. Numerous critics[120] have noticed how the knight seems to be
in a position analogous to his victim earlier: "take al my good and
lat my body go," he pleads with the Loathly Lady.[121] But "he /
Constreyned was," as his former promise to do as the hag wished
has bound him, and the knight marries the old woman.[122] One of
the things the knight is constrained to do is to consummate this
marriage with the old woman. Although the lady gives her famous
pillow lecture to try to convince the knight that she is as suitable
a wife as any, and more than some, in the end to fulfill his oath,
the knight must sleep with her. The choice she asks him to make
reminds him that he owes her a sexual debt in marriage, parallel to
the sexual debt she owes him. Sometimes the autonomy enjoyed by
husbands was technically constrained in ways similar to the autonomy of wives, as we saw in the example of Lucretia and Collatine.
In this instance, the *Wife of Bath's Tale* highlights the knight learn-
ing his agency-lesson when he submits his sexual autonomy to his
wife: "I put me in youre wise governance; / Cheseth youreself
which may be moost plesance / And moost honour to yow and me
also."[123] In this resignation, the knight also recognizes the union of
person that has occurred at one level between his wife and him. Her
actions, not his alone, play a role in determining their combined
"honour." Although legally the knight is primary, this compressed
discussion recognizes that the wife in a relationship can act alone
and separately from her husband, and that he may still be forced to
accept the consequences of that action as if it were his own.[124]

The Loathly Lady rewards the knight for his understanding of
the limits of husbandly autonomy by transforming into a beautiful, young woman, who will be both "good and trewe / as evere

was wyf," specifically including obedience, as "she obeyed hym in every thyng / That myghte doon hym plesance or likyng."[125] The knight has acknowledged the fact that the primary agent in marriage, the husband, is constrained, if to a different degree than the wife is. Linking the rape that began the tale to the knight's discontent at the constraint of his autonomy, in the *Wife of Bath's Tale* Chaucer uncovers the constraint of both the husband's and the wife's agency in marriage and contrasts it implicitly with the extreme lack of autonomy of the rape victim.

The *Weddynge of Sir Gawain and Dame Ragnell* parallels this exploration into marital autonomy by delving into the relationships involved in lord–affine relations (king–subject specifically). *Weddynge* is recognized as an analogue to the *Wife of Bath's Tale*, and includes the fraught wedding (this time of Gawain and Ragnell, the Loathly Lady).[126] However, the constraint Gawain finds himself in on his wedding night is linked directly to his relationship with Arthur, and the promise made to him, and his constraint as a husband is secondary to this primary relationship.

In the *Weddynge of Sir Gawain and Dame Ragnell*, it is Arthur who must answer the question of what women most want. When he stumbles upon Ragnell, she will give him the answer only if Arthur agrees to marry her to Sir Gawain. When Arthur goes to tell Gawain that he has an answer that will spare his life, but only at the expense of Gawain, Gawain agrees immediately to the marriage. Although a leaf of the manuscript is lost and so the beginning of the wedding night is missing from the text, where the manuscript resumes it is clear that Gawain has hesitated to consummate the marriage, just as had the knight in the *Wife of Bath's Tale*. The differences in what prompts the Lady's transformation in each text are instructive. Unlike Chaucer's Loathly Lady's double bind of being beautiful and unchaste or ugly and chaste, in *Weddynge* Ragnell reminds Gawain pointedly that he had promised Arthur, his lord, to wed her. Upon invoking a promise to his lord, Gawain turns immediately toward his new wife and agrees to a full measure of physical intimacy with her, whereupon she transforms into a beautiful young woman.

Whereas in the *Wife of Bath's Tale*, the knight's oath to the lady constrains him as a husband, here Gawain's oath to *Arthur* is the constraining element, and the marital debt a secondary element. "'A, Sir Gawen, syn I have you wed, / Shewe me your cortesy in bed; / With ryghte itt may nott be denyed,'" Ragnell complains.[127] She demands that he kiss her, at least, for Arthur's sake, and remember the demands of marriage.[128] Invocation of Arthur's name effects an immediate change on Gawain. No longer does he fight intimacy: "Sir Gawen sayd, 'I wolle do more / Then for to kysse, and God before!' / He turnyd hym her untille."[129] Gawain's relationship with Arthur is primary here in the sense of being an earlier bond, the promises of which must be kept before those of secondary bonds such as, in this case, marriage.

Gawain's autonomy, it seems, is already constrained, and this constraint suggests that we examine the agreement between Arthur and Gawain closely.

> "Gawen, I mett today with the fowlyst Lady
> That evere I sawe, sertenly.
> She sayd to me my lyfe she wold save—
> Butt fyrst she wold the to husbond have.
> Wherfor I am wo begon—
> Thus in my hartt I make my mone."
> "Ys this alle?" then sayd Gawen;
> "I shalle wed her and wed her agayn, / .... / .... /
> Her shalle I wed, by the Rood,
> Or elles were nott I your frende.
>
> "For ye ar my Kyng with honour
> And have worshypt me in many a stowre;
> Therfor shalle I nott lett.
> To save your lyfe, Lorde, itt were my parte,
> Or were I false and a greatt coward;
> And my worshypp is the bett."[130]

The bond between the two men is one of reciprocity. Arthur has helped Gawain "in many a stowre," and Gawain is entirely ready to return the gesture, even when the "battle" is a marriage. As king, Arthur has the power to constrain Gawain's choices, but he does not actively.[131] Gawain accepts this constraint on his own as a "frend," in response to his experience of Arthur's kingship, which includes Arthur protecting Gawain.

The agency relationship between a husband and a wife was complex, and this complexity is fully demonstrated in the literature. Authors used the contemporary institution of coverture to explore how these relationships might negatively constrain both the husband's and the wife's autonomy. Likewise, the analogous relationship of lord and servant (or retainer) is sometimes invoked. In all of these texts, if either party in an unequal relationship pressures the other party to do something they do not wish to do, that party may be constrained to do it. While this state of affairs may grate on our modern sensibilities, in medieval practice, these were honorable, indeed highly respected, relationships. If the actions each side constrained the other to take were legal and moral ones, then all was well, from a medieval perspective. It is when the actions were not legal or moral that the dangers inherent in these unequal relationships begin to be revealed, as we begin to see in the last two chapters.

CHAPTER 4

RETAINING MEN

Given the prevalence of unequal relationships between men in later medieval England and the honor attached to being in the highest levels of service, to neglect a consideration of the presence of retaining in late medieval English literature leaves our understanding of these works imperfect at best. Through literature, authors both echo and add to the parliamentary voices that historians have long examined as sources of information about retaining. Unequal relationships between middle- and upper-class men profited and affected a wide swath of society by the final years of the fourteenth century, yet authors came down strongly against retaining. But perhaps counterintuitively, the response gradually improved; by the eve of the Wars of the Roses, when retainer armies plagued the English political structure, poets extol the virtues of this type of service, even when they are clearly aware of its drawbacks.

Examples of retaining can be found in Chaucer, Langland, and Lydgate, among other Ricardian and Lancastrian poets. The seldom-read *Tale of Melibee* in Chaucer's *Canterbury Tales* is one of the most detailed discussions of a retinue in English literature, and will serve to illustrate what retaining looks like in texts. I will also investigate two other extended depictions of retaining in Ricardian literature: the Rat Parliament and Lady Meed's retinue, both from Langland's *Piers Plowman*. Through their use of allegory, these texts highlight the ethical tensions surrounding retaining. What appears to have bothered Langland most about unequal relationships was the way in which they could remove personal responsibility from the retainer for some of his actions. Nevertheless, by the early fifteenth century more hopeful views began to be expressed. *Richard the Redeless* demonstrates concerns about the pressures service exerted on loyalty, but at the same time suggests that if managed ethically, unequal relationships between men could play a positive role in the counties. By the second quarter of the fifteenth century, Lydgate explores royal affinities and concludes that they are overwhelmingly positive institutions. The Arthuriad in the *Fall of Princes* is based on the ideals of the Order of the Knights of the Bath. The Order emphasized those elements of judicial responsibility that the nobility and gentry, the classes most likely to engage in retaining, looked after in the shires. In Lydgate, the retinue of the Round Table itself is mobilized as a source of legal due process, disregarding common law and Parliament. While Chaucer and Langland took part in the critical fourteenth-century dialog also seen in documentary sources about the shape retaining was to take, Lydgate valorizes it in a move characteristic of the service-saturated fifteenth century. Chaucer and Langland explored the ramifications of this social institution with critical eyes. Lydgate had no choice; retaining, and with it, maintenance, was there to stay.

Chaucer's *Tale of Melibee* narrates a chain of events that was all too typical of fourteenth- and fifteenth-century England: offense, counsel-taking, and reprisal, and service culture and unequal relationships underwrite the entire tale. The crime at the beginning, an attack on Melibee's wife Prudence and daughter Sophia, is described in enough detail to satisfy the English legal system, and Chaucer emphasizes legalities at a number of points.[1] Once Melibee decides to respond to the attack on his house and family, he calls a council of advisors that Chaucer's medieval audiences would have recognized as retainers. The culture of service creates problems in Chaucer's text at every step; conflict between retinues may lie behind the initial violence, and Melibee's council takes their relationship with Melibee into account before counseling him to follow his own impulses.[2] Finally, the solution resembles the popular English out-of-court resolution method called a "loveday" or accord. Sadly, historically, the relationship between service culture and the popularity of the accord seems to have been strong and not always fueled by genuinely peaceful intentions. Service culture may well leave the peaceful resolution at the end of the *Melibee* in jeopardy.

Because social networks were a primary means of organizing local, regional, and sometimes even national power in late medieval England, Melibee calls on his immediately after his house and family are attacked, and illustrates neatly the double bind of the lord-retainer bond. The group Melibee surrounds himself with is a fictionalized cross-section of the social groups a lord might retain in either short- or long-term relationships. His "greet congregacion of folk" includes surgeons, physicians, and lastly, "wise advocatz lerned in the lawe": each of these groups engages in service of some sort, and it was common practice in the Middle Ages for surgeons, physicians, and lawyers to accept fees from noblemen.[3] In addition, Melibee calls to his council people who are not retained, per se, but nonetheless exist on the fringes of a service network: some of his old enemies with whom he had reconciled (or at least were "by hir semblaunt") some of his neighbors who respected him more out of fear than love, and flatterers. Even the kind of settlement ending the tale could create a bond between men not unlike that between lord and man. In addition, lords sought out alliances even with less powerful neighbors, as these neighbors might otherwise ally with the lord's enemies. Even if Melibee's neighbors fear him more than they love him, or perhaps *because* they fear him, the social hierarchy they inhabit compels their attendance.

Money is shown to be one motor of these relationships time and again, and Prudence takes for granted that a man of Melibee's stature and wealth must use money to draw people to him. As she says, "by richesses may a man gete hym grete freendes."[4] Melibee does not have a large group of blood relatives "wherfore that [his] enemys for drede sholde stinte to plede with [him] or to destroye [his] persone."[5] Instead, Melibee's "richesses mooten been dispended in diverse parties" before he can hope for loyal allies.[6] Medieval sensibilities promoted giving and receiving good counsel, but when Melibee's retainers proceed to counsel him, Chaucer makes it clear that his counselors' financial dependency on Melibee colors their advice to him. As Prudence points out, "the riche man hath selde good conseil" because "the counseillours of grete lordes / ...enforcen hem alwey rather to speken plesante wordes, enclynynge to the lordes lust."[7] Retainers tell the lord what he wants to hear, and after noting that "in herte [Melibee] baar a crueel ire, redy to doon vengeaunce upon his foes," few of these counselors fail to argue in favor of armed reprisal.[8]

The problem, of course, is that because all of these men are beholden to Melibee for something, whether money or future amicability, they are not able to function as wise counsel, and are leading Melibee toward legal wrongdoing. Prudence points the issue when she notes that Melibee "most *eschue the conseillyng of hem that been thy servantz* and beren thee greet reverence, for peraventure they seyn it moore for drede than for love."[9] Nevertheless, she notes also that some of the counselors gave good advice, and that they deserve a reward for their counsel, or they might be less likely to fulfill their duty to Melibee to the greatest extent possible.[10] She adds, "for al be it so that they been youre freendes, therefore shal ye nat suffren that they serve yow for noght, / but ye oghte the rather gerdone hem and shewe hem youre largesse."[11] As we saw last chapter, as a wife, Prudence is part of this system of unequal relationships too, and she acknowledges that biased counsel might still be useful, and should be rewarded as such.[12] Although it could conflict with their responsibility to provide good counsel to their lords, in some ways, being a yes-man *was* a responsibility of retainers: they were to support their lord's quarrels, even if doing so was illegal.

The debate Melibee has, first with his retainers, and then with his wife, results in the decision to hold a loveday or accord, a solution susceptible to the tensions inherent in service culture.[13] Accords were a popular means of out-of-court settlement because they were relatively fast and economical compared to the formal law courts. In an accord, both sides compromised in a settlement, and so they functioned to renegotiate power relations in a peaceful fashion that otherwise might have been settled more criminally.

Nevertheless, this very flexibility meant that accords were even more likely than the courts to be influenced by social networks, as we saw in chapter 2. Overpartiality on the part of the arbitrators or punitive settlements could easily lead to future trouble. Indeed, in 1393, a parliamentary arbitration agreement included a promise that neither lordship nor service would factor into the arbitration or its aftermath.[14] Biased settlements may even have been expected: "in practice, mediators could, and did, seek to impose partisan awards in the interests of kinship, friendship, 'good lordship' or even personal gain."[15] Parties to an accord could be pressured to settle or to act as arbitrators in order to maintain social status or reputation.[16] This bullying alone might be the goal of an accord. Thus, in choosing this means of conflict resolution, Melibee and Prudence recognize that peace can renegotiate the power relationship between Melibee and his enemies as well or better than war can. This loveday might be an antagonistic (and opportunistic) one. Carole Rawcliffe would agree that Melibee, Prudence, and their enemies may be hedging their bets: "although clearly successful on some occasions, such ceremonies were, on others, little more than an empty charade which provided the spectator with an interesting theatrical display but offered little in the way of positive results."[17] Although heading a less powerful retinue than his enemies, Melibee has won this round of the power struggle, but in doing so, exposed some of the significant limitations of unequal relationships.

Chaucer's *Tale of Melibee* introduces us to one way a retinue was depicted in literature and points to how service's dual basis, loyalty and finance, could further social trouble as easily as ameliorate it. Langland's depiction of Meed in *Piers Plowman* explores in detail how the reward and loyalty characteristic of maintenance influenced action, and links the relationship between lord and man with marriage. The two versions of the Rat Parliament segment reveal a development of Langland's thoughts on maintenance as he revised his text in the final decades of the fourteenth century.[18] The Rat Parliament and Lady Meed's retinue in *Piers Plowman* introduce unequal relationships into Langland's text as significant, and perhaps inevitable, problems in his "fair feld ful of folk."[19] Moreover, in making Meed lord of a retinue, Langland engages the core issue of how service, like marriage, functioned to transfer and regulate power between men. Chaucer expressed ambivalence about the roles of money and loyalty in retinues, but Meed embodies that ambivalence. Meed as a maintainer is nearly overdetermined, and in gendering her female, Langland asks bold questions about how service culture encouraged men to give up autonomy in the name of loyalty when it was convenient to do so, as we saw women did in marriage.[20] Furthermore, in the B and C texts, the presence of Meed's retinue in passus 2–4 is foreshadowed by an earlier debate, the Rat Parliament in the Prologue concerning livery, clothing characteristic of service.

Changes in the rat fable reflect the shifting political landscape of the later fourteenth century, especially as the debate about retaining changed.[21] Summarized briefly, the rodents in the Prologue of the B and C texts discuss how dangerous a particular cat is to them. A rat suggests giving the cat a collar with a warning bell on it, but when no rodent can be found willing to deliver the collar, a mouse recommends abandoning that tactic, submitting a further proposal that Langland revised between the B and C recensions. As had Chaucer, Langland depicted unequal relationships in his B text as having both beneficial and destructive qualities, but as Langland revised his text, he ceased to offer viable solutions for the negative ramifications. Instead of retaining the cat as the B text suggests, C leaves the small creatures resigned to living with an uncontrollable, dangerous power. Even in a fable, the lesser creatures cannot pretend to have the power to renegotiate a relationship with their more powerful neighbor. Neither service nor lordship will protect them.

One Langlandian character who service both enables and shelters is Lady Meed, who here is both female and, simultaneously, a lord of men. While there is some debate about whether Meed lacks agency, or acts with an overabundance of agency, many, including Stephanie Trigg and Elizabeth Fowler, recognize that the issue of agency is fundamental to passus 2–4.[22] Fowler outlines canon law's definition of the agency required in order to consent to marriage, and compares this type of agency with that recognized by the common law in property transactions. As we have seen in chapter 3, medieval society recognized a husband's legal coverture of his wife as a particular power dynamic on which other relationships could be modeled or to which they might be compared.[23] Fowler argues that the relationship between a king and his counselor functions as a near analogy to that between a husband and wife, and claims that the king "marries" Reason in passus 4, and that both escape civil death because both are men.[24] As we have seen elsewhere in this book, other relationships between men were also seen as analogous to the relationship between a husband and wife, underlining the commonplace and utilitarian nature of such maintenance dynamics.

Yet the theory of coverture was not always reflected in practice, as Stephanie Trigg demonstrates in her discussion of Edward III's notorious mistress, Alice Perrers. Trigg points out that both Perrers and Meed acted sometimes as *femmes couvert*, women under coverture of their husbands and legally inculpable for any civil misdeeds, and at other times, both the politico and the character acted as *femmes sole*, women with individual legal identity.[25] Following Fowler's argument, Trigg finds it significant that both Perrers and Meed served as royal counselors, and both controlled property and men. Meed is both passive and active: Meed accepts proposed marriages to both False and Conscience, and defends herself against Conscience's accusations.[26] Indeed, I would add that Langland employs Meed not just to probe the nature of coverture, but to explore actively another social relationship analogous to marriage: that between a lord and his man.

The 1377 impeachment of Alice Perrers provides insight into the connections contemporaries saw between marriage and lordship.[27] The previous year, the Commons had complained "that some women have pursued various business and disputes in the king's courts by way of maintenance, bribing and influencing the parties."[28] The Commons wished such lordly behavior by women, and "especially Alice Perrers" to be banned. This focus on Perrers

as an individual continued. Perrers is treated as a *femme sole* throughout the impeachment records, and this is both legally and politically significant. Had Parliament decided that Perrers was *femme
couvert*, and answerable to a husband or a father (or even an uncle
or a brother) complaint against her would have had to have been
made about a man, and would therefore have had a different sort
of political force. Alice Perrers' culpability depended on whether
she was considered *femme sole* or *femme couvert*. While her actual
marital state remains in question, obviously Parliament wanted her
guilty, and identifying Perrers as a lord of men, therefore *femme
sole*, and an analogue of a man, assisted in actualizing that desire.
To punish Perrers most thoroughly, she had to stand alone, stripped
of any possibility of the protective "unity of person" provided by
coverture.

A similar sort of unity of person can be seen within retinues:
history is rife with examples of retainers behaving illegally at their
lords' behests.[29] Unscrupulous retainers could commit crimes and
be confident that the service networks they inhabited would protect them from legal sanctions. Indeed, the courts were loud with
complaints against such retainers. Early statutes regulating livery
and maintenance were debated in Parliament and enrolled as statutes in 1377 and 1390, but enforcement proved to be sporadic.
Maintenance-at-law, or, "undertaking or sustaining any quarrel [in
the courts] by maintenance," was the concentration of this legislation, but the debate is only one sign of a growing concern about
service's potential to corrupt the legal system.[30]

These relationships, and the agency they conferred and enabled,
were complex. Both Meed and Perrers benefited from the autonomy
marking their participation in marriage and lordship. However,
Meed is also an allegory of reward, one of the motivations of service. Holy Church herself introduces Meed, Favel, and False's retinues as a "lordshipe," and in doing so she links Meed, marriage,
retaining, and the sliding agencies characteristic of those relationships. Moreover, Meed's slippery agency has roots in her ancestry.
If Meed is a "mayde," as Langland says, then she is under the coverture of her father, and Meed's father, False Fickle-tongue, himself

embodies the slipperiness of the *sole/couvert* continuum.[31] Meed has a duty to obey her father, although in doing so she disparages the character Loyalty. But she is not always a dutiful daughter: Holy Church also notices her out on her own, at the papal palace. Indeed, "the multiple, sometimes conflicting loyalties Meed demonstrates result from the flexible autonomy characteristic of unequal relationships."[32]

As I have argued elsewhere, in showing retainers acting as witnesses to the drawing up of the "feffement," Langland implies Meed's lordship over men.[33] Langland identifies the crowd at the reading of the marriage charter as "al the riche retenaunce," "on bothe two sides [both Meed's and False's retainers]"; clearly this is a combination of the retinues of Meed, Favel, and False.[34] Meed's retinue includes people found commonly in the localities. These men range from the nobler members of a retinue, like the "knightes of cuntre," to liveried menial servants of a great estate like the reeve and miller.[35] Langland increases the number of legal personnel in these retinues from A to B, adding sheriffs, bailiffs, and canon lawyers to the jurymen, summoners, and beadle found in A.[36] This "meyne" intends to travel to Westminster "to wytnesse this dede."[37] A sheriff and a juryman serve as absurd mounts for Meed and False, allegorizing a tension between the demands that these servants be loyal to their lords as well as their legal duties, and this image emphasizes the potential for loyalty to trump legality.

The importance of the marriage charter to these passages highlights the relationship contemporaries saw between marriage and service. In some cases, retainers received land from their lords in the same way as property was settled on a new husband and wife. Property transfer marked the new relationships in the community, and served as reminders of each side's responsibilities to the other. While married women were not able to hold property theoretically, Trigg points out that some did indeed: Meed seems to be one such property-holding wife, as the retainers closest to Meed witness her marriage charter.[38] In company with Alice Perrers, whether Meed is *femme sole* or *femme couvert* is determined by factors well beyond the letter of the law.

Ultimately, rather than travel to court, False, Favel, and the retinues flee, and the *visio*-king's understanding of how False and Favel may avoid imprisonment highlights similarities between marriage and service. If the pair are attached, taken into custody, most likely other members of their networks will "meynprise" them, bailing them, as it were. In an attempt to prevent this, the king denies them the option of mainprise while cautioning his men that False, Favel, and Liar are likely to attempt to use bribes or influence to avoid capture.[39] Service benefited both lord and retainer in this way: lord and man could escape punishment using legal devices like mainprise.[40]

In contrast to False and Favel, Meed is taken into royal custody, providing Langland a further opportunity to demonstrate her lordship. She finds that the judges arrive swiftly to curry her favor, and they are included in the group of new retainers when she gives, "the leste man of here *mayne* a motoun of gold."[41] Clerks and friars likewise come to Meed to attempt to gain favor and patronage. Retaining judges and clerks was still common practice throughout this period, despite a 1384 statute banning the practice.[42] Moreover, as the decades passed, it became more and more common for retainers to take fees from several lords. In the later recensions the clerks are quite aware of this development: if Meed cannot reward them according to their expectations, they will find lordship elsewhere.[43]

Langland is forceful in his denouncement of certain kinds of remuneration for service, yet expresses this position in a variety of ways across the A and B recensions, as though searching for the crux of the problem. In A the narrator says, "Ignis devorabit tabernacula eorum qui libenter accipiunt munera," and then relates the translation to service directly: "this Latyn amountith / That fuyr shal falle and forbrenne at the laste / The houses and the homes of hem that desiren / To have yeftis for here service in youthe or in elde."[44] Reward before or after a servant's tenure seemed like unearned reward: this was not "one pennyworth for another." In B, Conscience concentrates the translation on maintenance of officials: he cautions that those who desire, "yiftes or yeresyeves because of hire office" will find their houses burned.[45] Although referring to annual gifts generally, primarily a "yeresyeve," or "yearsgift," indicated "a gift as a reward for service, including both traditional livery, bribes, and promissory gifts."[46]

Unsurprisingly, service proves to be a significant topic in Conscience's thoughts about "mede" and "mercede," and the grammatical analogy of passus 3 as well. The Godly meed of which Conscience speaks is the correct form of remuneration: it is "mesurable hire" or "mercede."[47] Alternately, "mede mesureless" is dangerous, and associated directly with maintenance: lords "to mayntene mysdoers mede thei take."[48] As we saw above, an important concern is that "mede measureless" could occur before work was completed; "therefore, the relation between the work and the amount of payment is presupposed."[49] Reward incommensurate with work was the foundation of maintenance and the higher orders of service, and Langland explores this problem specifically in the complex grammatical analogy in the C text.

As I have said elsewhere, in the grammatical analogy, "'mercede' is associated with 'relacoun rect' while indirect relations are linked to meed and service."[50] Conscience argues that a solution to the difficulty would be for rulers to offer "lond or lordschipe oþer large yeftes" to loyal, well-performing servants only: these gifts would be repossessed in the case of disloyalty.[51] When the common people work for wages and the nobility demands loyal service from their retainers, right relations result. As we shall see, Langland was not alone in seeing this pattern of fee-for-services rendered as a solution to retaining's negative side.

In the end, Conscience associates indirect relations with the Parliamentary Commons, and especially legal personnel, and he sees both as problematic, encouraging more self-serving greed than interest in the common profit. When he says "þe moste partie of peple now puyr indirect semeth. / For they wilnen and wolden as beste were for hemsulue / Thow the kyng and þe comune al the coest hadde," I think Conscience identifies three groups, and not simply the king and the "comune."[52] I have argued that the "comune" may be identified with the Parliamentary Commons, but a third group may be singled out as particularly self-serving.[53]

The third, self-serving group is formed of those lords and their men participating in unequal, service relationships.

Support for identifying Conscience's critique of the self-servers with service culture can be found in the following harangue against indirect relations, which turns out to be a list of abuses associated with maintenance. Conscience concentrates particularly on embracery and maintenance-at-law: for example, "be the peccunie ypaied, thow parties chyde, / He þat mede may lacche maketh lytel tale."[54] Lords' purveyors left less cash than they owed, or even simply tallies, in place of adequate payment for requisitioned supplies, knowing that the power of their lord protected them from litigation over such extortion. An affine was well-placed to skim off the top of these transactions, as well as making his power over suppliers painfully clear. The double entendre in the next line, "nyme he a noumbre of noble or of shillynges, / How þat cliauntes acorde acounteth mede litel," refers "to those who hire lawyers coming to terms, [and at the same time] those same people may be 'clients' themselves, that is, retainers."[55] As we saw earlier in the chapter, Chaucer worried that lovedays might be more about peace than justice. Passus 4 finds Langland concentrating on this topic, when one of Meed's retainers needs her assistance.[56]

From leaving tallies to murder, the "wrong" perpetrated by Wrong falls squarely into the types of offenses retainers could commit with relative impunity. That Wrong is clearly one of Meed's retainers, as I have argued elsewhere, is evinced by her going to his aid both legally and extralegally when he gets caught. Meed offers to wage, or stand surety, for Wrong, and in so doing, demonstrates neatly how little separated the legal action of waging from the illegal one of bribery.[57] Passive until this point, Meed's first autonomous action finds her brokering reconciliation between Peace and Wrong, which "she does so by offering gold [....] as well as the promise of Wrong's future good conduct."[58] Here Meed follows John of Gaunt's recommendation to the Commons in 1384 admirably: lords should be responsible for their own retainers. Langland's contemporaries preferred out-of-court settlement to protracted litigation, as we saw earlier in this chapter, and Meed works within this preference. While Wrong remains in danger of legal punishment unless a mainpernor is found, Peace accepts the gift. Mainprise and waging appear here to vary little, if at all, from maintenance-at-law.

Just as Alice Perrers and Lady Meed share sliding agencies, the Rat Parliament provides an allegorical, political illustration of how some of the most powerful men in England sometimes did the same.[59] The shifting political landscape of the later fourteenth century, together with Langland's revisions, demand that we proceed with caution in attempting to associate historical figures with characters in the fable: "that the characters themselves remain the same simply highlights the palimpsestic nature of Langland's use of this fable."[60] The complex release schedule of what we know of as the B text that Warner has uncovered makes flexible associations of characters with political figures all the more necessary. For example, the cat may represent John of Gaunt, his son Henry Bolingbroke, earl of Derby, or even Richard II depending upon the recension.[61] The allegorical cat is a neighbor, another household animal, and a figure who was potentially an extraordinarily powerful competitor on both the local and national economic stages, and thus can be fitted to any number of possible historical persons. The rodents do their best to meet the cat's needs outside the household or county community, displacing him from their sphere of influence. In the end, the tactics the rodents use are characteristic of changes in the way retaining was practiced by the gentry and lower nobility in the later fourteenth century.

In the Rat Parliament, the rodents debate strategies for handling their cat problem, and they do so in ways reminiscent of the actual debates in Parliament concerning retaining. The cat acts "whan hym liked," and "at his wille," to the extent that the rodents fear to complain too loudly, least the cat "[pleie] with hem perillousli and [posse] hem aboute."[62] The cat's play with his rodent neighbors reminds us of how harassed human neighbors could feel, living near an overly powerful retainer. Indeed,

> Litigation was a common means to harass neighbors, and a powerful lord could easily "push around" those in his area [....] [P]rotoprerogative

courts such as the Court of Chancery were rapidly expanding in the later fourteenth century specifically because they heard cases in which a powerful defendant or his patrons obstructed justice for plaintiffs in lower, local common law courts until they dare not "grucche of his gamen."[63]

When one rat forwards the absurd solution of retaining the cat with the gift of a livery collar, the proposal recalls the complex power networks of service. This rat is familiar with retainers, or "segges," that remind us of dogs who, like the horses in passus 2, serve their lords faithfully: after all, both dogs and medieval retainers wore "beighes ful brighte abouten hire nekkes, / And somme colers of crafty work."[64] The rat notes approvingly that these retainers go "where hem leve liketh," and this tends to be "in wareyne and in waast," presumably far from the rodents' homes.[65] Retaining here is less an attempt to prevent violence than it is an effort to control it, to redirect it away from the rodents themselves, which in theory the bond of service would do. Clearly the cat is not imagined as feeling submissive to the rats, but as the Meed passus point out, the sliding autonomy available to retainers might prove attractive to the cat even so.

Inevitably, following the fable tradition, no rodent can be found who is willing to bell the cat, but the rodents do not rule out other sorts of gifts. A mouse suggest that it were better to offer venison to the cat than simply allow him to prey on them. While venison was a common gift in the Middle Ages, it was a lordly one: one had to be noble, or have ties to nobles, to have the rights to hunt deer. Of course a gift of food was clearly not as formal a token of service as the collar would have been, but nevertheless gift exchanges forged ties in medieval culture. The rodents wish to leave the cat in their debt with a gift of something valuable and high status in order to assure him that he is not "defamed" by an alliance, however tenuous, with the rodents.[66]

Both the rat and the mouse found possible solutions in service, a topic that Langland's London audience would have associated with John of Gaunt especially. In fact, John of Gaunt's prominence (or notoriety) in London lead to the burning of his Savoy palace

during the Peasants' Revolt.[67] Gaunt's livery collars received some
attention: just a few years before 1381, John Swinton's Lancastrian
collar nearly earned him a lynching.[68] The flexible autonomy of
such retainers rendered them as dangerous as the cat; the "segges"
are benign only to the power who can offer the sort of coverture of
a service relationship that the rodents hope to offer the cat.

Henry of Derby had a base in London too, and audiences might
also associate his men with the "segges" wearing collars.[69] Of particular interest, given how the "segges" are so like dogs, is Derby's
use of a collar of linked greyhounds.[70] Moreover, Derby's retinue
was associated with disorder during this period at least once: the
Cambridge Parliament dealt with a ravishment case in which some
of Derby's retainers were involved. Demonstrating that contradic-
tory blend of loyalty and lawlessness characteristic of good lordship,
Derby acquired a pardon for the ringleader.[71]

Of course there never was much hope for the rodents, and by
the C recension the mice and rats determine that there is no way to
ameliorate the feline threat. Indeed, they realize that if they get rid
of one cat, another will come along and take its place. In this recension, the cat may signify the King, in addition to Gaunt, Derby,
or the nobility in general. In 1390 Richard began to retain with
the badge of the White Hart, and as with all other retinues, those
bearing the White Hart could easily influence justice in the localities, as we shall see argued pointedly in the next section. Moreover,
such men were extraordinarily difficult to arrest or try, thanks to
the royal patronage they enjoyed.

Differences between the details of the B and C versions of the
rat fable seem to speak to ways in which the practice of retaining
changed over time. The trend among the nobility was to retain more
esquires, and fewer knights as the end of the century drew near; in
C the collars under discussion are worn in "cytees and townes" by
"bothe knyghtes and squieres."[72] The retainers in C are not likened
to dogs, and thus Derby's retinue is not singled out. Indeed, given
Richard's increasingly large, lowborn retinue in remote Cheshire, it
may have become impolitic to identify retainers with dogs roaming
the wilderness, and after these retainers began to sport the badge of

the White Hart, even allegorical gifts of venison might have been unwise. Of course, if Warner's theory of B's release postdating C's is correct, B's reference to venison becomes dangerously pointed. In any case, the mouse does not suggest feeding the cat venison in the C version; instead he advises to "soffre and sey nougt and that is þe beste."[73] It must have been a grim Commons who realized eventually that increasingly regulated retinues meant little if the king was exempt, free to build an affinity of lesser men, and John of Gaunt had the money and power to continue to maintain the largest legal magnate retinue in the land.

If Langland had to be careful in his criticism of service due to the precarious political milieu of the late fourteenth century, the author of *Richard the Redeless* could be strident, thanks to Richard's convenient availability as a cultural whipping boy when the work was written, in the early years of Henry IV's reign. As much as this text is an indictment of Richard's failure to rule well and an encomium for Henry, embedded within the poet's ferocious attacks on the Ricardian affinity must also be recognized an implicit criticism of Henry's own retaining practices. Retaining did not cease with Richard's death; in fact, the Lancastrian affinity grew from the largest noble retinue under Richard, to the largest royal affinity England had ever seen under Henry IV.[74] Any examination of the issue of service in *Richard the Redeless* must then keep one eye on the late Ricardian situation, and one on the developing Lancastrian government.

Throughout the fifteenth century, and in *Richard the Redeless* in particular, the cast of characters Langland depicts in the rat fable do not disappear; after all, the groundwork for early Lancastrian legislation concerning retaining and maintenance was laid down during Richard's regime. As mentioned above, John of Gaunt weathered Ricardian retaining statutes and persisted in supporting the largest single magnate affinity in England, second only in size to the king's. At Gaunt's death, this *familia* transferred its allegiance to Henry, and upon his accession, became a royal affinity, larger by far than any magnate retinue. The unparalleled resources of the House of Lancaster were now harnessed to royal ways and means. The practice of retaining in England would be changed forever.[75]

Henry's first parliament laid down strict rules about livery and maintenance that formed the basis for later statutes for much of the fifteenth century (1 Stat. 1 HIV c. 7 and 1 Stat. 2 HIV c. 21). Legislation like this helped Henry maintain order, and gave him the legal means to prosecute those who might attempt to oppose his new government by force. At the same time it acted as a public relations gesture to the Commons, who had voiced grievances against magnate affinities for decades. The king continued to have the liberty to retain at will any man above the level of yeoman, but retaining by others was greatly restricted. Moreover, unlike in previous statutes, a detailed system of enforcement was outlined; this royal monopoly on granting liveries was meant to last.

In this light, *Richard the Redeless* appears to be less of a violent-indictment-of-Richard-cum-cloaked-critique-of-Henry than it does a rather daring reminder to the new regime about the results of royal retaining practices. The author carefully edits the Articles of Deposition that lead to Richard's death to concentrate on service issues, and particularly those issues in which Henry IV's retinue might share. Yet, the fifteenth-century author sees good possibilities for noble retinues; poorly managed royal affinities and the maintenance of lesser men are the targets of his warnings. This is the first hint of a change in literary representations of this type of service.

That Richard is the negative model being invoked in *Richard the Redeless* is evident in the immediate evocation of the Articles of Deposition within the first dozen lines of passus 1:[76]

> *Radix omnium malorum cupiditas*
> Of alegeaunce now lerneth a lesson other tweyne
> Wher-by it standith and stablithe moste—
> By dr[e]de, or be dyntis, or domes vntrewe,
> Or by creaunce of coyne for castes of gile,
> By pillynge of youre peple youre prynces to plese,
> Or that youre wylle were wroughte though wisdom it nolde;
> Or be tallage of youre townnes without ony werre,
> By rewthles routus that ryffled euere,
> Be preysinge of polaxis that no pete hadde,
> Or be dette for thi dees, deme as thou fyndist,—
> Or be ledinge of lawe with loue well ytemprid.[77]

Each of these counts echoes an Article.[78] The "creaunce of coyne for castes of gile" calls to mind Richard's blatant sale of pardons treated in Article 24, and the infamous blank charters to which Article 38 referred. "Pillynge of youre peple, youre prynces to plese" recalls Article 43's complaint about the seizure of lands that were turned around and granted out to Richard's retainers. The poet's insistence that Richard had his will even when wisdom and good counsel argued otherwise reminds the reader of Articles 33 and 40 where: "when the lords of the realm, justices, and others, had been charged with faithfully counselling...the same lords, justices, and others, when giving counsel in accordance with their understanding were frequently rebuked and reprimanded, suddenly and so bitterly that they did not dare to speak the truth in giving their advice on the welfare of the king and the kingdom."[79] Taxation in time of peace was the subject of Article 32. The rowdy "routus" and the pitiless "polaxis" call to mind Articles 20 and 22, castigating Richard for the license he allowed his Cheshire affines.[80] "Or be dette for thi dees, deme as thou fyndist" suggests the attempts to avoid paying on crown debt described in Article 31.[81] The "loue" tempering law referenced in the last line sounds sarcastic. It suggests the direct corrupting influence of maintenance on the legal system, a problem noted throughout the Articles. One thing the *Richard*-poet does is to avoid the Articles dealing directly with Henry and the other matters specific to the 1399 revolution. Effectively, the list of articles begins as a warning for "kyngis and kayseris comynge hereafter," and is rendered into a specific warning for Henry to avoid Richard's mistakes.[82]

Passus 2 opens with the poet's special concerns about Richard's affinity: "moche now me merveilith and well may I in sothe, / Of youre large lyverey to leodis aboughte."[83] The poet characterizes Richard's affines as bearing "marks," "signs," or "broches" of the White Hart, references to the badges that the king began to distribute in 1390. The men bearing these signs are many, disturb the customary order of Parliament, and interfere in the legal system; all "bare hem the bolder for her gay broches."[84] The king has no need of a retinue, the poet argues, for all subjects are bound to him already: "for frist at youre anoyntynge alle were youre owen."[85] The royal affinity creates division in the country between those who have the king's favor and those who do not.[86] For all loved the king before liveries, the poet asserts: they "loved you full lelly or lyverez begynne."[87] Afterward, the "pouere / Lieges...loved you the lesse for [the retainers'] yvell dedis."[88] At higher levels of society, gentry and nobles denied royal service grew dissatisfied, as they saw lands and preferments pass to those bearing the White Hart only.[89] Royal affinities are in themselves dangerous for national unity, and anathema when not policed closely by their lord, the king. Moreover, it was quite clear that Richard's retainers were all too willing to hide their illicit activities under their royal lord's power.

Nevertheless, the poet argues for certain positive uses of livery, and in so doing departs from Chaucer's and Langland's negative depictions of retaining:

> Now for to telle trouthe thus than me thynketh,
> That no manere meyntenour shulde merkis bere,
> Ne have lordis leuere the lawe to apeire, / .... /
> But ho-so had kunnynge and conscience bothe
> To stonde vnstombled and stronge in his wittis,
> Lele in his leuynge, leuyd by his owen,
> That no manere mede shulde make him wrye,
> For to trien a trouthe be-twynne two sidis,
> And lette for no lordschep the law to susteyne / ... / ... /
> He shuld haue a signe and sum-what be yere
> For to kepe his contre in quiete and in reste.[90]

What becomes clear is that the *Richard*-poet disagrees with the retaining of middle men only, and this is consonant with the types of livery he does not discredit: liveried great men, livery of cloth, and livery collars.[91] These were men with enough personal wealth to support themselves, to "live of their own," and they would not be tempted to travesty legal cases for "mede" or because the opposing side was backed by a powerful lord.[92] Thanks to their ability to keep their counties in "quiet and rest," these already powerful men should be given a token reminder of their value to their king, in the form of a sign and a bit of an extra reward annually.[93] Neither a payment in expectancy, nor significant reward for deeds done, the *Richard*-poet sees royal maintenance as a gracious gesture of thanks and encouragement with little monetary value. Here there are no sliding agencies: the lords' desires are in harmony with the king's. This is important, because in a retinue headed by a king, legal influence became dangerously unpunishable maintenance-at-law, and a retainer acting independently of his lord could be seen as a traitor.

The *Richard*-poet recommends that Henry of Derby should practice such judicious retaining. The young deer that go without food while Richard feeds his chosen herd well are taken in by Henry, as a bird protects its chicks with its wings.[94] Moreover, we might read all the references to Gloucester, Arundel, and Warwick and their retinues by their signs (swan, horse, and bear, respectively) as evidence that the *Richard*-poet sees these lords as retaining correctly, or at least correctly compared to Richard. The poet emphasizes the monetary inducements that Richard offers his men, and how money cannot buy loyalty; in the end Meed has not prejudiced the loyalties of Gloucester, Arundel, and Warwick, who practice, apparently, "right relations."[95]

Retaining continued to grow as a social institution through the first half of the fifteenth century, assisted undoubtedly by the demands of the French war for troops, and of the minority government for political and social organization in the absence of a strong king. In the *Fall of Princes*, John Lydgate includes a positive depiction of a special affinity that capitalizes on legal technicalities in order to assist the judicial system, rather than subvert it. Henry IV's efforts to control magnate retaining have already been mentioned, but Henry V took the process a step further with a surprising innovation: he required all members of the royal affinity to swear to serve only the king, thus reinforcing the fact that this royal, Lancastrian lord could offer patronage equaled by no other.[96] Loyalty here was constrained, it is true, but the sliding autonomy that made service relationships so dangerous was also checked to a degree. One of Henry's retainers might act independently, but never under any lord other than the king, and never at cross purposes to him (or not at cross purposes for long). Although eventually pardoning malefactors, Henry policed the existing legislation closely. Although this royal control over retaining ended abruptly with Henry V's death, Lydgate's picture of Arthur's careful control over this special retinue of knights may have been meant for the young king Henry VI as a model recalling his father.

The *Fall of Princes* is a monumental work that took Lydgate most of the 1430s to complete, but within it, the Arthuriad serves to focus Book 8.[97] Before the Arthuriad, Lydgate translates a sermon on the conduct of kings that includes a section unique to Lydgate emphasizing the dangers posed to stable rule by duplicity and treason.[98] The only tie the Arthuriad has to the Roman history surrounding it in Lydgate's text is its brief recounting of Arthur's Roman campaign. While Arthur falls tragically, it is not out of any personal maliciousness or sin, but Mordred's treason. In fact, Lydgate's unique treatment of Arthur as the sun of England, worthy of stellification after being taken to Avalon,[99] makes the Arthuriad an unusually positive (and long) story in Book 8.

When the editor, Henry Bergen, noted that most of Lydgate's Arthuriad comes from his source, Laurent de Premierfait,[100] he downplays considerably how much Lydgate's original additions and his amplification of Laurent shift the focus of the Arthuriad. In Laurent, the story reads much like a compressed *Alliterative Morte Darthur*, where Arthur comes to rule over an England of plenty, refuses to pay tribute to Rome, conquers Europe and Rome, and dies defending his English throne from Mordred, who has taken control of England in Arthur's absence. In Lydgate, the prefatory material about England and Arthur's coming to power and the material about the Roman war are separated by nearly 150 lines devoted to the workings of Arthur's special affinity, the Order of the Round Table. We have seen how Lancastrian monarchs made greater and more often successful efforts to restrict retaining to the royal affinity alone than had Richard, and this made the chivalric orders, so dependent on royal patronage, appear even more like special branches of a royal affinity than they had in the fourteenth century.[101] The primary wartime duty of the higher levels of real affinities was military action, while their peacetime service centered (in theory) on keeping order in the counties, and so Lydgate makes sure that the Round Table's traditional presence in the Arthurian Roman War is balanced by its peacekeeping function at home.

First Lydgate outlines statutes comprising a list of duties the knights swear to perform.[102] Although an oath taken by the knights of the Round Table is found in Lydgate's source, it is a more abbreviated form that emphasizes chivalric honor.[103] Lydgate's oath is catelogic, and goes far beyond his source in detail, range of activities, and emphasis on the judicial nature of the knights' duties. Drawing from his source, Lydgate's knights promise to wear armor at all times, except when asleep, in constant readiness to accomplish knightly deeds.[104] They are to assist weaker parties, and do no violence.[105] From there, Lydgate develops his own theme. The knights of the Lydgatian Round Table are also to resist tyrants, protect widows, maidens, and wards, repatriate those exiled wrongfully,[106] and defend the rights of the Church.[107] In addition, these knights were to perform a sort of chivalric version of the Seven Corporal Works of Mercy.[108] All of these labors were to be done for the "comoun proffit."[109]

The only other Round Table oath in medieval literature is the Pentecostal Oath in Malory's *Le Morte Darthur* that critics believe Malory based upon the oath taken by the Knights of the Bath.[110] Be that as it may, Lydgate echoes the legal inflection of the Bath injunctions more so than does Malory, and reflects his familiarity with the Order of the Garter as well. The Order of the Garter originated with Edward III's desire to resurrect the Round Table, and that association should not be overlooked in discussing Lydgate's text. The duties of Lydgate's Round Table knights were ordained by *statutis* found in their *registre* (a book of laws), and "a clerk ther was to cronicle al ther deedies, / Bi pursyuauntis maad to hym report."[111] All of these references recall the register listing the ordinances of the Order of the Garter, and the records of its doings set down by a "register" or clerk, who by Lydgate's time was informed by a herald (a pursuivant was a lower level of herald).[112] The Order of the Garter was a significantly different organization than the Knights of the Bath, however, and while links exist between the Round Table and the Garter, Lydgate goes to great pains to associate the Round Table knights with those of the Bath.

The antiquarian John Anstis could find no records of the Knights of the Bath as such before the reign of Henry IV, but the practice of soon-to-be-knighted soldiers engaging in a formal ceremony including bathing was much older.[113] Indeed, the custom seemed to have emphasized the creation of Knights of the Bath at coronations of new kings; therefore the new king and the new knights were raised together, and the knights formed a special cadre of royal affiliates. A description of the ceremony of knighting roughly contemporary with the *Fall of Princes* included the following injunctions to the new knights:

> ye schall love god above all thinge and be stedfaste in the feythe and sustene the chirche and ye schall be trewe un to yowre sovereyne lorde and trewe of yowre worde and promys & sekirtee in [f.196b] that oughte to be kepte. also ye schall sustene wydowes in ther right at every tyme they wol requere yow and maydenys in ther virginite and helpe hem & socoure hem with yowre good that for lak of good they be not mysgovernyd. Also ye schall sitte ī noo plase where that eny iugement schulde be gevyn wrongefully ayens eny body to yowre knowleche Also ye schall not suffir noo murdreris nor extorcioners of the kyngis pepill with in the Contre there ye dwelle but with yowre power ye schall lete doo take them and put them in to the handis of Justice and that they be punysshid as the kyngis lawe woll.[114]

The knights' duties to protect the economic rights of widows are emphasized, as is the necessity of protecting the physical and financial rights of virgins, and the duty to work within the legal system to bring order to their counties. The legal uses to which Lydgate's Arthur put his affinity echo these injunctions closely.

Both the Bath ordinances and Lydgate's statutes focus on ways the knights should use their power to aid people prejudiced by an imperfect legal system. To emphasize royal affinities, and the chivalric orders in particular, reinforced the Lancastrian tendency to make retaining as much of a royal monopoly as possible. Recall that the Lancastrian kings were the most lucrative lords a retainer could have in a double sense, as scions of the House of Lancaster, a noble family since the fourteenth century twice as rich as any other, and as kings. Retainers of any other lord might share class status with a royal retainer or member of a chivalric order, but they did not share the same wealth or prestige, and Lancastrian-sponsored texts like the *Fall of Princes* highlight that fact by concentrating on the elite retainers exclusively. Moreover, to link licit assistance in the judicial process with maintenance forced royal retainers to align their personal actions in the localities with their lord *and* king's wishes. Failure to do so was not simply to contradict one's lord, but to contradict one's king, and therefore treasonous.

Throughout the Arthuriad, Lydgate focuses on the legal aspects of each of the duties that Arthur's affinity promises to accomplish. Lydgate concentrates on the ways widows and maidens are legally challenged by linking widows and maidens with wards, and he identifies all three as groups that were understood to be discriminated against under the law. The knights are to see to it "that widwes, maidnes, suffre no damage / Be fals oppressioun of hatful cruelte, / Restoren childre to ther trewe heritage."[115] A child who lost a father who had held certain kinds of land became a ward of the king, and the ward's patrimony, the *heritage*, would be controlled by his or her royally appointed guardian until the ward reached legal age. Wards often found it difficult to acquire control of their patrimonies; sometimes it proved impossible.[116] The Bath injunctions recognize how difficult widows could find it to enter into their portion after their husbands' deaths, and also recommend that knights take less well-off virgins into their financial protection in a manner similar to wards, in this case, by making sure they had the financial wherewithal to make good matches and avoid being "mysgovernd." An "oppressioun" could refer to almost any trespass or felony, and maidens (unmarried women) and widows faced hurdles similar to those faced by wards in taking and retaining possession of property that had been bequeathed or otherwise conveyed to them. They might all need assistance to "restoren [them] to ther trewe heritage."

Lydgate concentrates his prolixity on reiterating how these "widwes, maidnes, oppressid folk also" received assistance, and implicates the knights in some legal maneuvering of their own.[117] Arthur's knights are to spend their time "rihtful quarellis to susteene & diffende": that is, they are to prosecute other mens' quarrels, in other words, practice maintenance-at-law.[118] Here Lydgate departs radically from the Bath ordinances' careful insistence on due process.[119] The poet repeats this recipe for justice wherein knights maintain others' rightful quarrels several more times in the same section. In one of the repetitions Lydgate elaborates on how the knights are to accomplish this legal aid: "as riht requereth, ther quarelis to *darreyne*."[120] As Richard Firth Green has pointed out regarding Chaucer's *Knight's Tale*, "darreyne" was a special legal term referring to trial by combat, a relatively rare form of judicial proof that nevertheless appeared to be on the increase in the late fourteenth and fifteenth centuries.[121] Lydgate kept Arthur's knights within the law, but only just.

In a manner of speaking, trial by combat was legally sanctioned maintenance-at-law: although practiced in the common law in theory, by the fourteenth century, judicial combat was the province of the noncommon law Court of the Constable and Marshal, otherwise known as the Court of Chivalry. In trial by combat, both plaintiff and defendant could name champions to fight the battle for them. As Lydgate describes it, knights "shal ay be reedi to susteene that partie, / His lyff, his bodi to putte in iupartie."[122] However, according to statute, the Court of Chivalry was to act only in cases where the common law did not hold: in cases originating overseas, for example, or with cases arising from military matters like ransom or indentures.[123] Clearly, complaints such as withholding a ward's inheritance stood well within the jurisdiction of the common law. Nevertheless, in practice, and despite Parliamentary complaint, the Court of Chivalry became a popular platform on which to prosecute any grievance involving breach of faith in the late fourteenth century, and it continued to decide cases outside of its formal jurisdiction in the fifteenth century.[124] For Lydgate to argue *for* increased use of the Court of Chivalry, and for a wider acceptance of the most dramatic form of maintenance-at-law, by depicting it as standard practice in Arthur's model government is both a radical reimagination of legal procedure and a stern reminder of the role knights played, for good or ill, in local administration. Lest we think Lydgate too monkish to dabble in such cynicism, we might consider that he was among the first Englishmen to demonstrate, in his *Fall of Princes*, an understanding of "pollecie," a term with connotations similar to real politik.[125]

In short, in his Arthuriad, Lydgate sets up royally administered maintenance-at-law as a positive model. The poet emphasizes that Arthur himself assigns knights to individuals who come to his court to "pleyne," that is, make a formal plea against an offending party. In one instance any wronged party "sholde fynde a kniht / To hym assigned," and in another, anyone in need of legal succor "foorth anon[e] riht / Then to diffende asigned was a kniht."[126] If this is still for the "comoun proffit" as Lydgate said earlier, we might look on these knights as the public defenders of the Arthurian legal system, "by marcial doom his quarel to diffende."[127] Lydgate is a long way from the Ricardian statute outlawing this very practice. Nevertheless, in promoting this style of government, Lydgate was outlining a strategy similar to that practiced by the Lancastrian regime under Henry V. Henry was a strong king, and worked not simply to curb retaining, but to make it the sole province of the king. Lydgate moves this image of a strong ruler surrounded by a singular retinue into Arthurian legend, and recasts the Bath ordinances into the Arthurian world of the *pas d'armes*. Instead of handing criminals over to royal courts, Arthur hands out his knights to the dispossessed and those against whom the law was prejudiced.

It cannot be coincidence that as England moved again toward civil war, literary depictions of retaining balanced the positive potential of the institution against the probability that retinues would be used solely for personal gain.[128] Already in the 1430s, Lydgate looked back to a mythical golden age of Henry V in the guise of King Arthur. Not until Edward IV did a monarch successfully work to enforce statutes predating Henry VI's long and troubled reign: the new 1468 Statute of Liveries continued to be the statute concerning retaining most often enforced until it was superseded in 1504.[129] There is consensus among historians that by the later fifteenth century, nonroyal retinues were smaller, and other means of expressing power and patronage were becoming common.

In the final chapter, I will examine more closely a topic touched on throughout this chapter: the influence of unequal relationships on the judicial system. As we have seen, medieval people were quite aware of the dangers that the complex loyalties required in service relationships could exert in legal scenarios. Although the author of *Richard the Redeless* and Lydgate expressed hope for positive uses of retaining, John Gower and Thomas Hoccleve exposed the means by which unequal relationships corrupt the legal system fundamentally through the service provided by legal officials.

CHAPTER 5

MAINTAINING JUSTICE

Starting in the 1370s, both ethical and practical dissatisfaction with the maintenance system began to be voiced from within, from the most protected retainers of all, the lawyers, and early essays into solutions began to be made. The lawyer John Gower[1] and the bureaucrat Thomas Hoccleve made radical claims for the role of legal professionals that integrate the issues of retaining and autonomy that we have been tracking throughout this book. Gower begins in the 1370s by insisting that legal professionals are immoral if they exert their own discretion over the working of the law. Gower expresses concern for the lack of oversight of the legal profession, and implies that perhaps more regulation would curb abuses fundamental to a legal system embroiled in maintenance. By the 1390s his claims regarding the unimpeded movement of the law became even more far-reaching, and he insisted that the special judicial decision-making powers residing in the person of the king must be exercised only through delegation to his legal and judicial officials, in an effort to provide oversight over even the king's judicial prerogative. The practice of "laboring" and biased viewpoints characteristic of service culture that we have seen in previous chapters were beginning slowly to be questioned, although obviously change took time to be effected. Once the shape of the problem came to be outlined, solutions began to be proposed. In the 1410s, Hoccleve argues that bureaucrats have special expertise with which to critique the laws and legal system, thus providing an answer to the question of professional oversight posed by Gower.

Having a bit more background in the intricacies of fourteenth-century England's jurisdictional system will assist in understanding the arguments made by the authors covered in this chapter.[2] Speaking generally, common law was practiced through central, royal courts such as King's Bench, Sessions of the Peace and Courts of Assize, and Common Pleas, or through local courts such as county and hundredal courts in the provinces. By the late fourteenth century, professional lawyers monopolized legal proceedings at all levels. An attorney (*attornatus, atturne*) entered pleas and made complaints for his employer in court; legally they were the same person, and the litigant was constrained by his or her attorney's actions. A pleader (*narrator, placitator, causidicus, conteur, pledour*) made the oral argument in court on behalf of the litigant or the attorney, to which argument the litigant could add or disavow. Technically, most pleaders in most courts were apprentices; only about a dozen at a time were admitted to the bar in the Court of Common Pleas, where they held a monopoly on pleading and by the 1370s were known as serjeants-at-law (*causidicus, pledour, serjeaunt*). Judges were appointed exclusively from the pool of serjeants-at-law by the fourteenth century.

Critique of the legal profession was not new in the late fourteenth century, but the way late-fourteenth-century critics attempted to assess the problem and begin to propose solutions was new. Developments of the late-fourteenth-century legal profession and methods of remuneration are reflected in a change in authors' approaches. Providing us a baseline is the roughly 160-line section of the *Speculum Vitae* that concentrates on the law.[3] The author, William of Nassington (d.1359) provides us with example of an earlier critique that depicts the problem of corrupt legal officials as a simple one, usually based in greed, rather than a complicated one with roots deeply embedded in social and cultural conditions that demanded complex solutions. Nassington's discussion of legal officials serves as his example for the fourth branch of the sin avarice, and he does note toward the end that he "spoke anely of fals men / ... / .... / And noght of þam þat trewely dothe."[4] Nevertheless, the passage that precedes that caveat details ways that nearly every participant of the legal process might influence its outcome unethically. Throughout, Nassington reveals only the means of corrupting due process, not the motives the officials have for their malpractice except for the overarching one of avarice.

While Nassington includes the very base of the legal structure, plaintiffs and defendants, the balance of his critique falls squarely upon legal professionals.[5] He begins discussing sheriffs and bailiffs as a transition from his earlier section on robbery. Lumped together, these officials have real power over people's physical bodies, after all, "þai prison þam and doþe þam shame / and fetteres þam and doþe þam payne."[6] Nassington claims that only by making a large fine to the sheriff and bailiff could a person get out of jail literally. The depth of selfishness Nassington associates with this practice, so prejudiced against the poor, he says, "semes a manere of robbery."[7]

After sheriffs and bailiffs, Nassington turns from the topic of robbery to that of "chalenge," a word denoting a claim, either false or true. This felicitous theme allows Nassington to discuss both false claims brought by legal officials, and the true claims against their wrongdoing. His estimations of various legal positions are short, and sometimes curiously unemotional: for example, "also þe fals sissour is prest / Þat gangs opon a fals onquest / þat puttes a man fra his right tyt / Thurgh schowyng of a fals verdit."[8] The danger of the more learned lawmen is their ability to "turne right into wrange," an allegation we shall see that Gower also makes.[9] This is a hazard with lawyers in general, and each specialization accomplishes it in its own way. Pleaders were the lawyers who made the arguments in court. A pleader could begin unjustly by taking up a false plea, but he could also fix cases by creating unnecessary delays, misleading the inquest jury, or giving false evidence.[10] Most disturbing, the pleader can hide his misdeeds so that "his falshed may men noght wele knaw / Ffor he can couer it with þe lawe."[11]

Attorneys and judges highlight two of the issues dealt with throughout this book, unequal agency relationships, and the changing mechanisms of remuneration. An attorney can follow a wrong plea instead of a right one, just as the pleader can, according to Nassington, but because an attorney acts as the proxy for his employer, his crime is especially heinous if he deliberately loses the case: then he becomes a traitor, as well as an oath-breaker.[12] Under the Statute of Treasons (1352), the crime of petty treason was created so that a wife killing her husband, or a servant his master were each traitors. Just as a wife could serve as her husband's proxy because they were the same legal person, an attorney shared a more limited version of this legal personhood, acting as his client's proxy in court. Meanwhile, judges err primarily by accepting bribes from both sides, and determining the case for the side with the largest gift.[13] In addition, judges can collude with jurors who have loyalties to one side or the other; the jurors can advise that the judge give a false judgment or force a delay in the trial.[14] This is the only place where Nassington acknowledges the influence of outside parties on legal officials.

Although Nassington does not point out reasons for this corruption directly, he alludes to a motivation by placing this critique under the heading of avarice, a particularly economic sin, and by linking it to robbery. Nassington implies that the jurors, lawyers, and judges misdirect justice for financial reasons, but he does not go further into the issue than that. In the most recent comprehensive study of legal officials and payment, J.R. Maddicott and others remind us that lawyers and judges were part of a culture in transition: legal professionals began the *cursus honorum* as counselors for their lords and were bound to them through the complex ties explored in previous chapters.[15] Judges and lawyers could be among the retinues of the great (as we saw in the letters of chapter 2), or they could be hired on an ad hoc basis. Gifts exchanged could be diverse: for example, cash or hospitality over the holidays. In the case of judges, these perquisites easily surpassed the legislated salary, payment of which was often in arrears. Money was never the entire issue, however. As Maddicott says, "to see the relationship of justices...and their clients merely in financial terms was to simplify a situation which had become very complex"; furthermore, "a prohibition on fees, robes and gifts could hardly undo relationships which could find expression in other ways and which had other sympathies at their roots."[16] We might recall the complex relationship between Brian

Roucliffe, Third Baron of the Exchequer, and William Plumpton, discussed in chapter 2, here. While Plumpton was a significant man in his county, Roucliffe's position gave him national standing, and despite his son's marriage with Plumpton's granddaughter, Roucliffe continues to address Plumpton, one of his employers, with deference.

Beginning in about 1370, however, ties between judges and the nobility began to be a political issue on a scale not before seen. While Maddicott sees this move as part of a larger fight against inefficient government, by this point I think we can also see it as part of a parallel debate about fictions of autonomy: who did the legal professionals serve? To whom was their autonomy surrendered? The king? The lords of their retinues? Their employers? Or, perhaps, the law itself? The evidence suggests that social and cultural changes were at work as much as legal changes: a reinstated statute limiting judicial gift-taking was *repealed* in 1386, and salaries of judges were doubled in 1389 to 110 marks, a significant salary.[17] Nevertheless, as Maddicott himself admits, the networks that bound legal personnel were not purely financial. The mid-fifteenth-century letters we examined in chapter 2 alone demonstrate that legal professionals continued to be tightly enmeshed in service networks well after 1390.[18]

An exploration of the literature of the late fourteenth and early fifteenth century allows us to complicate Maddicott's thesis, exploring a growing concern with retaining and the law, and at the same time revealing the fundamental connection between the two for the medieval English. While the parliamentary records Maddicott studied demonstrate a concern for the disorder and violence judicial malfeasance promoted, literature allows us to delve more deeply than that, and examine one of the mechanisms for this disorder, unequal relationships. As his oeuvre spans the decades Maddicott discusses, it is no surprise to see Gower's works developing an increasingly complex understanding of the problem of autonomy and legal corruption over time. Having lived and worked through some of this time period, and writing at the beginning of the fifteenth century, Hoccleve extrapolates even further and thanks to his own personal situation, may suggest a solution that might work for everyone, as it seems to have worked for the judges in the fourteenth century: regular, sufficient payment of a salary. Nevertheless, he does so still as a putative member of the king's household.

In his earliest long work, the *Mirour de l'Omme*, dating to the 1370s, Gower lays out a number of specific problems within the legal profession, and expresses serious concern with the ad hoc nature of payment procedures. Furthermore, when it came to the law, *all* maintenance began to look like bad maintenance; it *all* seemed to encourage corruption within the profession. In subsequent works, he continues to develop this theme, relating the practice of the law to personal autonomy and influences on that autonomy. The *Vox Clamantis* dates to the late 1370s and early 1380s, and refocuses its section on lawyers, borrowed from the earlier *Mirour*, on how money changes hands around the law. No critic has heretofore examined the apparently odd juxtaposition of Gower's critique of lawyers in Book 6 of the *Vox*, itself an unusual addition to an estates' satire, with a letter addressing the king.

As the lawyer and historian Edward Powell put it, "above all, justice in the late middle ages was a co-operative enterprise involving the king and his people," and for Powell, these people are lawyers.[19] Critical to understanding this combination of Mirror for Princes with Mirror for Lawyers is the topic Gower uses as a transition between the two: the judicial role of the king. I argue that Gower promotes the free movement of the law through the medium of the common law, unconstrained by noncommon law courts based on the king's lone prerogative. This scenario gives significant power to the legal profession, and necessitates that the profession identify what constitutes professional ethics, and then practice them. These are the very topics Gower pushes so hard in the earlier passages borrowed almost to a word from the moralistic *Mirour*.

Here we have two moving targets, the constantly developing legal system, and changing cultural perceptions about what role laws and lawyers should play in the legal system. Gower assumes that his audiences understand certain things about "the law": justice should be impartial and be available to both rich and poor. Furthermore, although "ne puet savoir qui n'ad apris / Du loy les termes ne les ditz, / Tout pourrons nous le droit savoir" ["No one can understand the terms and expressions of the law unless he has studied them, but we can all know the right"]: here Gower implies that despite the trappings of the legal profession, at base it should reflect a fundamental "droit" that we all can recognize.[20] To bring Leicester's vocabulary in once more, Gower is most definitely in favor of *laying down the law* on these matters, if he could only determine how to do so. Unlike Nassington, Gower does reach some conclusions, however: according to Gower, legal officials can only justly serve their clients by using their delegated powers, rather than relying on their own discretion to determine cases, and similarly, justice will only be served if the king continued to delegate his own decision-making powers to legal professionals.

Gower characterizes the legal estate with two words, *tort* (wrong), and *fort* (strong).[21] Echoing Nassington, the wrongs of lawmen extend especially to avariciousness and how their work can seem to twist the law. Although Gower castigates all "gens du loy" often enough, the group he singles out within this larger category are the pleaders (*pledours, causidici*); he never refers directly to attorneys. The poet is most concerned in the *Mirour* with lawyers' financial gain from their work, as well as how a lawyer can make a successful suit even for a client who is in the wrong: "qe ja n'ert droit si apparant / Qui contre tort ara guarant, / Qant ils ont la querelle pris" ["No right is so obvious that it can prevail against wrong when they take on a case"].[22] Moreover, pleaders give no advice without prepayment, but will work for anyone who fees them, whether noble or not. Gower claims ignorance about whether or not the delays lawyers seem to encourage in cases are legal or not. In addition, for some reason, the poet darkly notes, the lawyers get out of paying taxes, and Gower portrays the lawyers as working against the common good by reducing funds (*bien commun*) available to the king.

Lawmen are also *fort*, however, both because of their professionalization and because of their usefulness to the great men of society. Gower grumbles that it is impossible to sue a lawyer, since the profession "ne pledont, ce diont plat, / L'un contre l'autre... / Ensi se sont *confederat*" ["For they say flatly that they will not plead against each other. Thus have they leagued together"].[23] Confederacy was a hot issue in the later fourteenth century, when the term was applied to a wide range of groups that legislators felt were using benefits of membership to unfair advantage.[24] We might recall the mob analogy from chapter 1 when we read that Gower depicts lawyers as petty thugs using their legal knowledge as a weapon with which to shake people down: "mandant ses briefs pour faire entendre / Qe s'il n'ait part de leur florins, / Il les ferra destruire ou pendre" ["Sending his briefs to make them understand that unless he gets part of their money he will destroy them or have them hanged"].[25]

While Gower rails at lawyers' fees, he asserts that the judiciary determines only for the litigant offering the largest bribe (*doun, munera, dona*), immediately throwing judges' impartiality into question.[26] Within the first few lines of the *Vox*, Gower expresses this sentiment this way: "hic labor, hoc opus, est primo cum munere iungi" ["(Lawyers') work and effort are primarily to be connected with their (gifts)"].[27] Like bribes, intercessory letters (*lettres a prier*) sent by nobles on behalf of litigants sway judges' decisions. *Amour* can also corrupt judges, and Gower notes how difficult it is to sue a case against anyone who has ties (*amy, alliance, lignage*) with the judge. Finally, Gower notes that sheer intimidation (*doubte*) renders judges useless: they fear determining against nobles. Corrupt judges are a particularly vicious travesty of the legal system, since they have power over life and property. However, as Nassington noted, sheriffs and jurors controlled life and property, too, sheriffs through selection of jurors, and jurors by swearing to the rightness of a defendant's plea and delivering presentments (similar to indictments) to the court. Parliamentary records demonstrate the Commons voicing a desire to regulate the judiciary more closely especially from the mid-1370s, and the issue of judicial interest became a pressing one as concern was expressed over feeing and bribing judges and jurors.[28]

Longer by far than the section on judges, though, is the section following on sheriffs, bailiffs, and jurors.[29] Gower repeats the fact that sheriffs take an oath to uphold the law, and both times he emphasizes that this oath is at least partially owed to the people (*communalté*, *pueple*). Like other men of law, sheriffs are guilty of improperly enriching themselves. Although Nassington criticized sheriffs too, Gower explores the mechanisms of corruption further. For example, sheriffs influence local decisions through purchased juries: the sheriff selects jurors likely to take bribes. Gower blames sheriffs, as he had lawyers, for causing delays in due process. Rapacious sub-bailiffs are next on Gower's list, but he links these tightly to corrupt sheriffs: "je croy que si de sa partie / Visconte fuist d'oneste vie, / Ly soubz baillif fuissent meillour" ["I believe that if a sheriff lived honorably, his (under) bailiff would be better"].[30]

Sheriffs and bailiffs aside, Gower, like Parliament, reserves special vitriol for corrupt juries. Just as he had earlier suggested that a bribed sheriff would lead to bribeable jurors, so in these passages Gower explains this process further. If the head juror (*capitein*) was amenable to bribes, he was a *traicier*.[31] Gower even describes the enculturation of novice jurors: until they learned to say as the *traicier* did, they posed a potential risk to his activities. Not only is the perjury of the *traiciers* dangerous for justice, but it potentially destabilizes the social order. Gower claims he lives near such a juror-for-hire and that the man lives and supports his family from his perjury. Finally, Gower complains that men who could genuinely swear to the truth of events fail to appear at court, either because they feel powerless against bribed jurors, or because they fear to dishonor their family names.

The conundrum that Gower puzzles over in the *Mirour*, and later in the *Vox*, is one of payment for services rendered. "Iceste gent... / Pour ce qu'ils ont la loy apris, / Par resoun duissont loy tenir / Et sustenir en leur paiis / Les drois" ["Because they have learned the law, these people...ought reasonably to keep the law and to uphold right in their country"] identifies the law as a profession requiring training, and also carrying with it responsibilities.[32] This distinction is important, as it figures the law as a service profession where a practitioner is held responsible not simply to himself, but also to his clients, and in this case, to the law itself. However the law was a peculiar kind of service, as "the law" had a "thingness" about it, and so perched uncomfortably between commodity and service.[33] Gower accuses pleaders of being whores, like Meed in *Piers Plowman*, and being "as comyn as þe cartway."[34] Yet, the poet accuses the lawyers of a false exchange of which whores are not guilty: he remarks succinctly that you may give a lawyer money, but "nil tibi retro dabit" ["He will give you nothing in return"].[35] Emphasizing the partial, personal decisions corrupt pleaders were willing to make, Gower likens lawyers to those who falsify scales in commercial transactions: "Pondere subtili species venduntur, vt emptor / Circumventus eo nesciat inde forum; / Est tamen ecce modo pondus subtilius, in quo / Venduntur verba legis in art sua" ["Wares are sold by delicate weighing so that the buyer, tricked by this, may not know the market value of them. But behold, now there is an even more delicate weighing process, through which the words of the law are sold in their own way"].[36]

Medieval English society wished to regulate its market quite closely, establishing by statute regular weights and measures, and sometimes even legislating prices for goods and services.[37] Lawyers represented both sides of a case, and winning and losing lawyers both got paid for their work. But how much? A client in the wrong who wins his case seems to get more for his money than a client in the right. A lawyer's fees either diminish a client's profits, or increase his or her losses. And how could it be right for both sides to try to win the case? The problem for Gower was both practical and theoretical. If law was a commodity, its exchange for money depended on quantity, and no set standards of "amounts of law" existed, and if it was a service, few regulations existed providing protections to consumers. Somewhere between a good and a service, the law seemed more than usually exempt from enforceable regulation.

The law did benefit from regulation, but when compared to the regular Assizes of Bread and Beer, lawmen faced official censure only rarely. While Brand notes that the Statute and Ordinance of Conspirators both mention lawmen, he contends that the Statute may be a draft, and the Ordinance provides for no method of enforcement.[38] The sole enforceable statute concerning legal misconduct dates to 1275, Westminster I, Chapter 29:

> it is provided also, That if any Serjeant [*sj'eaunt,*] Pleader [*cõtour,*] or other, do any manner of Deceit or Collusion in the King's Court, or consent [unto it,] in deceit of the Court, [or] to beguile the Court, or the Party, and thereof be attainted, he shall be imprisoned for a Year and a Day, and from thenceforth shall not be heard to plead in [that] Court for any Man; and if he be no Pleader [*cotour,*] he shall be imprisoned in like manner by the Space of a Year and a Day at least; and if the Trespass require greater Punishment, it shall be at the King's Pleasure.[39]

Chapter 30 also specifies that officers (*sj'aunz*) are not to practice extortion. Baker shows that while this statute was used to prosecute attorneys as well as serjeants and pleaders, litigation of any kind was rare.[40] Although these guidelines about personal misconduct provided a kind of quality assurance, it was a partial one indeed. Importantly, the value of the lawyers' work was never regulated; neither this nor subsequent statutes tried to restrict prices. Legal fees remained at the mercy of market forces, and the services provided received little consideration as well. One might be forgiven for a cynical suspicion that the lawyers, who benefited from a free market and participated in Parliament as MPs and counsel made sure that, in Leicester's words, the law was never laid down on this matter.

This left legal professionals to find remuneration where and how they might, and they turned to the full range of options provided by their culture. Clients were charged all the traffic would bear, and then some, as Gower makes clear throughout this section. For example, consider the persistent claims that the poor can get no law because they cannot afford to pay as much as the rich, although "poor" could be a relative term.[41] *Douns*, or bribes, were another option, and Gower notes these as especially a problem with the judiciary.[42] Another path to remuneration was the *alliance* or *seigneurage* that could fee legal officials as part of a retainer.

It seems that during Richard's reign, retaining lawmen ceased to be as attractive to lords as it had been earlier. Baker calls attention to the fact that "the retainer of men of law was expressly excepted from the legislation against maintenance and liveries"; nevertheless, he suggests that by the third quarter of the century, the notion that lawyers served the law itself rather than particular clients may have been developing, an expectation that I argue Gower demonstrates.[43] We might think about it in analogical terms. When a lord provided his man with an estate office, such as stewardship, the man drew remuneration from that office as long as his lord found his service adequate. In this worldview, a legal professional would expect to draw money from his position, too. However, if the legal professional's "lord" became the law itself, then adequate service became a theoretical notion, and an ethical position, in a different way than it had when the judge's lord had been a human being. Nevertheless, as we saw in chapter 2, and as Biggs argues from documentary evidence, when it came to supporting life and career, legal professionals continued to have recourse to service.

If *Piers Plowman* demonstrated how Meed must offer to wage her retainer Wrong in order to fulfill her duties as a lord, despite seeming to offer a bribe in so doing, as we saw in chapter 4, then Gower shows how the legal profession was in a similar double bind. If Langland's character Conscience had pointed out that the problem with retaining was that the lord pays the servant before he performs his duties, rather than after as a reward, then Gower notes with disapproval that lawyers are paid before they accept cases.[44] Gower recognizes that even normal business transactions put lawyers at risk of questionable practices: "Mais ove le riche ont leur conspir, / Et pour sa cause maintenir / Justice et loy mettont au pris" ["They conspire with the rich; and, in order to win their case, they put a price on the justice and law"].[45] As Gower hints with his single, economical sentence, a lawyer ran into ethical problems if he took his fees after a case as well. Maintaining others' quarrels in court, or maintenance-at-law, formed a portion of the legal definition of conspiracy and Parliament specifically complained of it in 1388.[46] The Ordinance of Conspirators defined and prohibited champerty, anyone suing a case for someone else with their own money in return for a share in the profits of a case, as well.[47] In this way, Gower points indirectly to the problem of unregulated legal fees, since in some ways lawyers were trapped. If a lawyer took fees after a successful case, he could be viewed as a champertor; if he accepted fees before a case, he might seem to be maintained. In either case, by accepting remuneration, the lawyer could be construed as acting unethically. In the *Vox Clamantis*, however, Gower adds another piece to the puzzle: he links the judicial practices of the legal profession to those of the king, a connection Powell sees as characteristic of the late fourteenth century.

In Gower's England, the king himself could be considered a man of law, and therefore Gower's arresting placement of a discussion of the ills of the legal profession next to a manual on good kingship is both logical and original. In the *Vox*, pleaders are juxtaposed with judges, sheriffs, bailiffs, jurors, and finally the king himself, suggesting that Gower is using some ordering principle that culminates with the king. This group of representative men of law are the king's appointed officials, and it is to the king that Gower turns after castigating his legal colleagues in the preceding *speculum causidicorum*. Ultimately, Gower's message seems to revolve around the relationship of the king to his legal officials and the law with which they work.

As he moves into the *speculum regale*, Gower turns to emphasize the impossibility that the king's subjects will behave well, if the king acts unjustly. Porter sees Gower following the *speculum* tradition in promoting individual good governance as a means to political right rule; Gower pushes this goal hardest in Book 6 of *Vox Clamantis*.[48] Speaking of the *speculum principis* in Book 7 of Gower's later work, the *Confessio Amantis*, Porter says: "Gower's treatment of [...] justice stresses the crucial connection between the king's need for ethical self-governance and the attainment of harmony within the body politic."[49] Ferster sums up the importance of Gower's *speculum regale* in the *Confessio* thusly: "Gower's work...help[ed] to make the language of advice part of political discourse, honing it as an instrument for criticizing the king."[50]

In ignoring his responsibility to practice justice, Richard was enabling dangerous tendencies already present in an unregulated legal marketplace. When the king failed to delegate his judicial decision-making power to the professionals, he implicitly encouraged them to use their own. In this way, the emphasis turns from the legal professionals of the last six chapters to the king himself. Consider "curia que maior defendere iura tenetur, / Nunc magis iniustas ambulat ipsa vias: / Infirmo capite priuantur membra salute, / Non tamen est medicus qui modo curat opus" ["The high court which is obligated to uphold justice now (more than ever walks unjust ways itself). When the head is weak, the bodily members are deprived of health, yet there is no physician who now takes care of our need"].[51] Here the legal profession appears wayward due to lack of sufficient royal guidance; they wander headless. As I will discuss in closing this section, this attitude corresponds closely with criticism of Richard as early as 1390. The law is paramount: "gens sine lege quid est?" ["What is a people without law?"] Gower asks.[52]

The king's active participation is necessary to the healthy functioning of the legal system, but equally crucial are members of the legal profession. Within the first few lines of the *speculum* Gower directs the king to recognize his role in the kingdom's law: "regis et est proprium, commissam quod sibi plebem / Dirigat, et iusta lege gubernet eam" ["And it is proper for the king to guide the people entrusted to him and govern it with just law"].[53] "O rex, ergo tue tua legi debita solue" ["O king, pay your debts to the law"], Gower pleads, "sis pius et populum dirige lege tuum" ["be dutiful and govern your people according to law"].[54] I think this symbiosis between the king and the legal profession, in which both king and lawyer must apply the law but not act upon it, is a key element of Gower's final message to Richard.

Gower asserts the dangers of the king's personal agency being used too directly as a judicial tool, and he locates this assertion squarely within the late-fourteenth-century political milieu: "iudicii signum gladius monstrare videtur, / Proditor vt periat, rex tenet arma secus: / Rex iubeat tales laqueo super alta leuari, / Ne periat Regis legis et ille status" [the sword is seen to make known the badge of justice, / so that the traitor may perish, the king must wield his arms otherwise: / the king should order such men raised up high by a noose, / so his status and the royal law does not perish].[55] There is no doubt here that the law originates with the king: the law is specifically his, "Regis legis." The threat to this law are those misusing both their military power and the "iudicii signum," or "badge of justice," which even the king could corrupt. As we saw in chapter 4, "signa," livery badges, were a contentious issue throughout Richard's reign. A common complaint was that retainers used their badges to facilitate intimidation and extortion, as well as more violent crimes: their swords became their badges of justice literally, since no one dared challenge them.[56] To combat this misuse of judicial authority, Gower insists that the forms of common law be obeyed: men who abuse the king's law are traitors and must be hanged, not executed summarily and in an unlawful manner, even by the king. Exercise of the king's ability to make judicial decisions appears here to be dangerous to the functioning of both the law and social order in the form of the king's status: he "must wield his arms otherwise," implicitly through the common law, and therefore its officials. Attention to the forms of the common law protects both the status of the king and the king's law itself. The revised version of the end of Gower's epistle to the king in Chapter 18 shows the necessity of the free movement of the common law to be one of Gower's primary messages.

Gower's revisions to Chapter 18 are consonant with Middleton's opinion that late-fourteenth-century critics thought that law and government, in the form of Parliament, not the king, should be "active" rather than "custodial" in regard to social concerns.[57] According to the revised version of Chapter 18, dating to sometime in the early 1390s, the king's proper role in relationship to the law was administrative, not participatory, and the chapter focuses overwhelmingly on the king's relationship to the common law. The poet acknowledges that the king's personal decision-making powers were unique and necessary in the preface to the chapter; nevertheless, Gower sets quickly about curbing this privilege within the common law. The king's discretion, his power to judge and make decisions, could be dangerous if it was clouded by personal concerns: "si rex sit vanus, sit auarus, sitque superbus, / Quo regnum torquet, terra subacta dolet" ["If a king is vain, greedy, and haughty, so that he torments his kingdom, the land subject to him suffers"].[58] Instead, the king must concentrate on actively developing a just legal system: "rex sibi commissas regni componere leges / Debet, et a nullo tollere iura viro" ["A king ought to weigh carefully the kingdom's laws, which are entrusted to him, and he ought to withhold justice from no man"].[59] The royal discretion must be exercised: "perdita restaures *communia iura*, que leges / Ad regnum reuoca" ["Restore our common justice, now lost; bring law back to the realm"].[60] The law originates with the king, but as his reference to "communia iura" demonstrates, Gower guides Richard carefully away from exercising his discretion as a kind of law unto itself: "dumque [suas] leges mixtas pietate gubernes, / Cuncta [sue] laudi gesta feruntur ibi" ["And as long as (he) administer(s) laws tempered with righteousness, (his) every action will redound to (his) praise"].[61] Moreover, Gower's concerns with how the king employed his personal discretion in public, judicial ways correspond with others' critiques of Richard in the 1390s.

Richard II's judicial role came under special scrutiny in the early 1390s. In 1389, he regained control of his government following the Appellant crisis of 1388, and for a time seemed to be living out Gower's recommendations for strong administration with little direct involvement in suits himself. The king promised to provide better access to justice, and his actions of the following months seemed to prove his commitment. He reappointed Commissions of the Peace with an eye toward legal competence: judges and serjeants were appointed at the expense of lords and knights. In contrast to the Appellants' delinquency, Richard moved swiftly to enforce the provisions regarding judicial salaries, powers of determination, size of commissions and nomination of Justices of the Peace and sheriffs made in the Statute of Cambridge of 1388. Sheriffs in 1389 were chosen by the king himself. No longer were these officials appointed by the Chancellor, Treasurer, Keeper of the Privy Seal, and Barons of the Exchequer. Nevertheless, by 1390 Richard began to cave in to baronial interests and by 1391 there were rumblings of dissent once more, making Gower's revised chapter a timely reminder of the king's previously stated intentions.[62]

In fact, in the early 1390s, Richard could be said to be "fashioning [. . .] a more assertive, more legalistic style of governance."[63] Richard's most recent biographer, Nigel Saul, sees him as no less obsessed by his judicial authority in the 1390s than he had been earlier, in the 1380s: "overriding all other objectives was to be the defense and maintenance of the powers of the prerogative."[64] In the 1390s, Richard may have been attempting very deliberately to live out the supreme royal prerogative described by Giles of Rome in his *speculum principis* , a text steeped in the civil law of the continent. This context throws Gower's *speculum regale*, especially its revisions, into full relief; Book 6 of the *Vox Clamantis* might function as a common law counterargument to the civilian promotion of royal authority espoused by Giles. Saul notes that contemporaries themselves noticed Richard's interest in civil law with some concern.[65] Gower does point out that doctors of civil law make good counselors, but this single positive remark seems drowned out by the body of Gower's pro-common law argument.[66] As a response, Gower tried to cajole the king back toward a less personally active administration of the common law, promoting the delegation of royal judicial power. Moreover, in setting aside his personal preferences, Richard would serve as a just model for those legal professionals who employed that power that the king had delegated to them: legal personnel were to handle the law, not act upon it.

Throughout the final quarter of the fourteenth century, Gower elaborates on baseline criticism like Nassington's, and hints at the problems stemming from lack of regulation, but he stops short of suggesting solutions below the level of the king himself. A decade into the fifteenth century, Hoccleve knew what a solution would be, at least for himself. Hoccleve's repeated pleas for payment situate the *Regiment* within the traditional genre of begging-poetry, but Hoccleve desires payment for his *bureaucratic* work, not his poetic undertaking, a point critics often overlook.[67] In both direct and indirect ways throughout his text, Hoccleve repeats that a ruler must listen to the advice that the experienced professionals around him give, and must pay them promptly and regularly for their labor. For purely personal reasons, then, Hoccleve presents a solution to the puzzle plaguing authors discussed throughout this chapter: to prevent legal professionals from improperly exerting their own discretions over the law, monarchs needed to recognize the profession for what it had become, a contractual, economically based relationship between an employer and an employee. Hoccleve sends the *Regiment* as a sort of bill for royal service he has rendered. In the rest of the chapter, I will map out how Hoccleve describes the intersections of the traditional service culture, and newer, more bureaucratic styles of professional payment. As we have seen, Chaucer and Langland explored these areas as well, and Gower even hints at a solution to the problem of retained men of law and industry regulation, but Hoccleve is the earliest, strong voice to provide a solution.[68]

Hoccleve was reacting to fairly new developments in professional bureaucracy. Some documentary evidence corroborates that this time saw a shift in perception of the royal clerks. For example, although Privy Seal clerks lived together in a hostel provided for them by the Keeper of the Privy Seal, it was only in 1409 that the legal fiction ceased to be maintained that this was a temporary measure until room could be found for their lodging within the king's household.[69] In fact, regular salary was not an innovation, but, according to Hoccleve's way of thinking, a method whose time had finally come. Royal clerks received a regular salary under Edward III, but later this strategy fell out of use so that by Hoccleve's time clerks were reliant upon small fees clients were supposed to pay and special royal rewards only. Nevertheless, despite Hoccleve's plan, it should be noted that after Henry IV, few annuities were granted, and so even this source of income dried up for the clerks, who became entirely reliant on fees and favor.[70] Hoccleve proves that solutions were conceived, even if implementation had to wait for a later point in history.

The relationship between the prefatory Dialogue with the Old Man and the *Regiment*-proper forms an important interpretive crux in Hoccleve criticism.[71] Although it is considered commonly from a confessional vantage,[72] a more useful perspective for my reading is offered by those critics considering economic angles.[73] Nicholas Perkins notices an economy where words are exchanged for money in the *Regiment*.[74] He shows that this theme is explored in particular in the Dialogue with the Old Man. On one hand, Hoccleve gives examples from Privy Seal life demonstrating how their work prevents speech, and on another, he shows that the flattery of lords' men leads to inflation in this economy of words, resulting in false exchanges of words for money.[75] Certainly in his discussion of lawyers and their lack of regulation, Gower shows a similar economy at work in his oeuvre. Perkins provides a thorough exploration of the exchange of words for money in the Dialogue with the Old Man, but does not credit Hoccleve, as a professional, with developing as unique a solution to his problems as I believe he does. *Nemo* is the patron of the Privy Seal clerks, as Hoccleve and Simpson point out; clerks are nobody's men.[76] Yet, I argue that this is precisely the point; clerks are not really part of a household or a retinue.[77] Instead, the clerks, including Hoccleve, are in the process of becoming working professionals, and the tie that binds them is the desire for a regular paycheck.

Several critics note how the Old Man seems to be a sort of "alter-ego," to use Scanlon's term, for Hoccleve, and I think this is a useful way of thinking about this portion of the text.[78] I suggest that we think about Hoccleve making his characters present different kinds of solutions to his problem, solutions that might have seemed equally valid in different ways to the bureaucrat. The Hoccleve-character voices contemporary concerns, and eventually a contemporary solution, while the Old Man voices traditional, no longer viable, solutions. If we do this, we can see the conflicting impulses pulling at the real-life bureaucrat who was trying to solve a real-life problem. Ingeniously, Hoccleve resolves the differences between the Old Man's suggestions and the contemporary situation that the Hoccleve-character inhabits in a literary product that is at once both traditional and situated tightly within the culture of the early fifteenth century, the *Regiment of Princes.*

Even the apparently unrelated discussion of apparel offers an opportunity for Hoccleve to contrast traditional household service with the poet's proposed solution. "What is a lord withouten his meynee," the Old Man asks, referring to the absence of clear delineations between ranks in clothing, but also to the relative poverty nobles found themselves in after spending so much on clothing that they could not afford to retain men: money "waastid is in outrageous array, / So that householdes men nat holde may."[79] To the Old Man it seems obvious that a lord should love his men more than his clothes.[80] Hoccleve's disinterest in complaining about his clothing affirms his emphasis on the professional, rather than household character of his work, since Privy Seal clerks were supposed to receive annual gifts of clothes from the king.[81] It's the missing cash payments, in other words, salary, that Hoccleve complains about, not missing clothing.

Hoccleve deftly plays with the language of service, only to reject it as an insufficient solution: "the lak of olde mennes cherisshynge / Is cause and ground of al myn hevynesse."[82] After this statement, Hoccleve continues to explain what kind of "cherisshynge" he has in mind, and it is not that of a retainer. The poet is a clerk in the Office of the Privy Seal and Henry IV had granted him an annuity, so in a sense, he is a royal retainer already, but it is difficult to make sure the money is paid.[83] Hoccleve never mentions a household, as the Old Man had in the previous lines, but aligns his profession with other skilled employees of the Crown.

Hoccleve draws parallels between his own problem and that faced by knights and men of arms who had been awarded annuities following campaigns. In fact, Hoccleve links these two professions closely: just as soldiers risk their bodily health in the field, so too do bureaucrats' bodies slowly succumb to the repetitive stresses of their jobs so that neither is any longer fit for other manual labor.[84] In a long description of his work, he points out that although some people think "that wrytynge / No travaille is," in reality, "it is wel gretter labour than it seemeth."[85] Mind, eye, and hand must all work in close concert for a clerk, and unlike craftsmen, he cannot talk, sing, or play while he works; a clerk must concentrate entirely on his task at all times.[86] Furthermore, Hoccleve points out the physical toll that writing takes on its practitioners; stomachs, backs, and eyes all wear out in time.[87] Here we see the total submission to the law that Gower called for among legal professionals, and hear a professional attest to the pride he has in doing his work without exerting his will over it, either to make it physically easier, or to make it more lucrative.

The comparison between the military and bureaucracy is instructive, as in the 1410s Lancastrian administration was experimenting with a new form of military. By the fifteenth century, soldiers were normally hired on an indenture, an early form of contract, that specified the duty to be performed, length of service, and amount and timing of payment. Remuneration was supposed to be regular. In the 1410s and 1420s Henry V led efforts to tighten this system, in part by developing a system of muster and review that allowed contracted terms of payment to be better met by both soldiers and commanders.[88] We should consider how professional Lancastrian armies were (or were supposed to be) when we speculate about the expectations bureaucrats like Hoccleve might have had of their employers.

The problem was really one of "identity economics"; Hoccleve and the bureaucrats in government service, like the soldiers in Henry's armies, would have been considered part of the king's household just generations before. Yet, by the fifteenth century, tradition no longer reflected economic or social reality, and traditional forms of maintenance were failing to provide adequate remuneration for these men. As Hoccleve says, "service [...] is noon heritage."[89] It was known that Henry IV granted more annuities than the Exchequer could cover.[90] Although the system was still attempting to follow traditions of payment based on the household, Hoccleve portrays himself as a professional, serving the king *and* the law. Only one of these masters could pay him. As we saw in previous chapters, if a lord failed to fulfill the agreement between himself and his man, the man was free to go.

The subject of patronage leads Hoccleve to complain about a common practice in the Privy Seal that demonstrates how the clerks were forced into dependence on collecting small fees from clients, and how retaining put the clerks at a disadvantage. If a plaintiff decides to take a case to court, he or she will find "sum lordes man" to sue it out for them.[91] This retainer comes to the Privy Seal and has the clerks write up the necessary forms, but then, instead of paying them the fees tradition required, he turns to another traditional form of payment, favor.[92] The retainer insists that his lord will thank the clerks, for "if [the clerks] han to sue to the kyng, / His lord may there have al his axyng. / [The clerks] shul be sped as fer as that [their] bille / Wole specifie th'effect of [their] wille."[93] Hoccleve understands that these offers function more as threats than as rewards, since any complaint the retainer makes will be believed, regardless of its veracity, and it "hard is be holden suspect with the grete."[94]

Hoccleve uses the Dialogue with the Old Man to establish the tensions that pull at the entire text. As much as the Old Man, and perhaps the author himself, wishes that traditional solutions to social and financial problems would work, both recognize that they no longer do. Hoccleve works throughout the rest of his text to manipulate traditional genres and traditional means of remuneration to meet his new, contemporary needs. Although he shares many exempla in common with Gower, we shall see how he mines these stories for material to forward his plan of getting paid in a way that Gower does not.

A number of the stories that Hoccleve chooses to tell Henry focus particularly on the interactions of a king or ruler with the judicial system, or with one of his employees or retainers. Hoccleve borrows most of his *exempla* from Jacobus de Cessolis' *De ludo scaccorum (On the Game of Chess)*,[95] and de Cessolis' stories fit Hoccleve's message well. Jacobus de Cessolis emphasizes the importance of communication between ruler and ruled in his chess analogy, and I believe that Hoccleve does the same.[96] Moreover, as de Cessolis makes clear, due to their experiences as subjects, the ruled may be privy to knowledge that their superiors are not, and have a duty to express that knowledge, thus going a step further than Gower's insinuations in *Vox Clamantis*.[97] Finally, the king uses his royal discretion correctly when he rewards subjects with payment for their services. The context of new bureaucratic professionalism that Hoccleve has established since the beginning of his text focuses de Cessolis' *exempla* on bureaucrats and legal personnel especially.

Examining a few of the *exempla* that concentrate on legal personnel will give us a good sense of Hoccleve's strategy. For a story centered on a king punishing an unjust judge, little has been written about the Judgment of Cambyses *exemplum* in relation to the legal profession. The story is a short one. A Persian judge develops a personal hatred of a particular man, and sentences him to death. When the king (unnamed in the *Regiment*, but called Cambyses in other versions) hears about this travesty, he orders the judge flayed alive, and his skin is used to cover the seat where the malicious judge's successor, the judge's own son, was to sit in judgment.[98]

Scanlon deals briefly with Gower's version of the story, presented in *Confessio Amantis*, by saying that "in this tale, the rule of law becomes identical to the king's unlimited capacity to carry out punishments in its name."[99] Dealing with Hoccleve's version of the tale, Perkins notices the *exemplum*'s emphasis on the body, where "ruptures in the body politic find solutions...in the physical bodies of its members"[100] I argue that this *exemplum* represents also the problem of remuneration of legal personnel, especially considering the fact that Hoccleve continues to discuss the problem explicitly for six stanzas before beginning another *exemplum*.

By implication, the Cambyses *exemplum* begins an investigation into the remuneration of the judiciary.[101] Although the judge is motivated by "wratthe and hate and the irous talent," the greater context in which Hoccleve situates the story may have reminded readers that in other versions, the judge accepted a bribe before handing down his final sentence.[102] The stanzas of criticism following the *exemplum* do not support Maddicott's belief that complaint over judicial bribery calmed after the 1380s. Hoccleve's complaints sound much like those heard from Nassington and Gower. Judges pass sentence out of interest, rather than impartially.[103] Receiving payment after an impartial decision was still considered to be wrong.[104] Hoccleve believes many judges decide for the party offering him the most money.[105] In this section, the bureaucrat echoes the double-bind in which Gower places lawyers: they are either maintainers or champertors depending on whether they take their fees before or after a case. Even more obviously than in Gower's work, Hoccleve insists that judges must be held accountable for the impartiality of their decisions. The bureaucrat implies the solution through his own request for a salary: judges will be less likely to take bribes or act incorrectly on their own volition if they receive a regularly paid, adequate salary.[106]

In the *exemplum* of the king, the fool, and the recidivist, Hoccleve models a king receiving and acting on good counsel delivered by a royal servant with special insight into human nature granted to him by his professional career. He begins by discussing a bit of Aristotle: "that for noon ire [Alexander] nevere be so hoot / Blood of man shede."[107] Instead of making this an enjoinder against emotional outbursts, however, Hoccleve corrects it on legal grounds: "but this nat ment is by the cours of lawe / That putte a man to deeth for cryme."[108] The specific lines that refute Aristotle and upon which Hoccleve expands for his following *exemplum* are "and if a kyng do swiche murdrers grace / Of lyf, he boldith hem eft to trespace."[109] A Latin marginal heading to this *exemplum* locates its force directly in contemporary legal politics. The marginal "nota contra concessiones cartarum pardonationum de murdris" [Note against the granting of charter of pardon for murders] makes specific reference to the notorious charters of pardon that could be purchased by and for criminals.[110] These documents acted as a kind of silencing of protest; communities could use the legal system to convict criminals, but could not always make convictions stick. The murderer in the story had gotten a pardon for his first homicide, and then committed another. Claiming that his highly placed friends can win the king's pardon for him again, the recidivist brags that "and they that now annoyen me or greeve, / I shal hem qwyte heereaftir, as I leeve."[111] As long as a criminal could receive royal pardons repeatedly, he could "qwyte," or settle with, his adversaries in any way he saw fit, legal or not.

When the recidivist arrives to request a charter of pardon from the king, the "fool sage" standing by the king denies that the criminal killed a second time. Rather, the fool asserts to the king that, "he slow him nat, for yee yourself him slow."[112] The fool points out that "if that the lawe mighte his cours han had, / This man heere had been for the first man deed," the second would never have been killed, and finally, that an unpunished felon would likely kill again.[113] The king sees the wisdom in his fool, and denies the recidivist a second pardon: "the lawe him gaf that longid to his meede."[114]

Hoccleve himself can be considered a "fool sage."[115] Hoccleve spends many lines of the Prologue and *Regiment* proper bemoaning his foolishness, but simultaneously he demonstrates that he does know his business, and that means bureaucratic business. Moreover, the problem of excessive pardons would be one of which Hoccleve would have special knowledge: charters of pardon were issued from the Chancery, but the royal warrants that ordered the Chancery to write up a charter were issued normally by the Privy Seal.[116] Thus, a Privy Seal clerk may well have recognized recidivists as their names repeatedly came under his pen, and certainly he would have been aware generally of the number of pardons being issued.

Emphasizing the significance of this problem, Hoccleve spends an additional four stanzas commenting on charters of pardon, and how the king does not do well to assert his own discretion over convictions by granting a pardon. He reiterates that unpunished criminals are likely to commit further crime. Furthermore, executing a single murderer can save more than one life, so that more honor accrues to the legal system sentencing him than to a sovereign pardoning him. Generally, pardons "al to lightly passe and goon," helped on their way by powerful men.[117] According to Hoccleve, only in the case of "oon be by malice of his foos / Endited" can a king demonstrate true pity and pardon a homicide honorably.[118]

True pity and honorable ruling is taught too in the *exemplum* of Caesar and the solider, an *exemplum* that demonstrates the responsibility rulers have to their employees as the scale tips from household servant to bureaucrat or employee. Hoccleve tells of a knight of Caesar's who finds himself about to be sentenced to death.[119] The knight cries out "with an hy vois, for to save his heed, / To his lord Cesar.../ Byseechynge him that, of his gracious might, / He wolde him helpe and reewe on his estat."[120] The knight thus invokes Caesar's obligation as the knight's lord, and hopes as well to trade on the emperor's power over the law. Initially Caesar acts as the sage fool of the earlier *exemplum* would have wished: he sends the knight "a good advocat," or lawyer.[121] The knight is not content with this, however, and speaks insubordinately to Caesar, reminding him of how much he has helped the emperor in his campaigns. "And advocat ne sente I noon to yow," the knight says; critical here is the role of the attorney as a proxy for the litigant in English law.[122] Just as a victim would display his or her wounds, the knight bares his scars in open court to prove his loyalty, to prove that his own body stood for the emperor's. Caesar grants the knight his point, and serves as the knight's advocate himself: "thus [Caesar] this knyght his deeth saved fro."[123]

So what makes Caesar's actions appropriate, and the earlier king's unwise? Hoccleve does not point out the knight's innocence, merely that he escapes execution. The answer, I think, is twofold. Caesar is not misusing the royal judicial powers as the other king was: he steps in as an attorney, a regular member of courtroom procedure.[124] Justice is not being sold in this story as pardons were. In addition, I think this later *exemplum* demonstrates some of the power relations Hoccleve advocates between lord and subject. The knight is successful in getting the king to recognize his duty to his employee. The knight's experience as a loyal soldier results in his ability to pressure Caesar into helping him directly in court, in another example of the complex relationships we have examined in several chapters now. The knight's service to Caesar is written on his body, and gives him some claim to his lord's attention. As we saw earlier, Hoccleve, too, notes how his own body has been marked in his bureaucratic service. Service begets service, as Caesar in turn *serves* as his knight's attorney, as his proxy.[125] Fulfilling his side of the mutual obligation proves to "the peple" that Caesar is not "a prowd man" or "ungentil."[126] Since Hoccleve has already drawn parallels between bureaucratic work and military labor, with this *exemplum*, Hoccleve suggests that his work for the Lancastrian Privy Seal has earned him his employer's assistance in fulfilling a financial need that may require legal power.

The final *exemplum* I want to discuss is the last in the *Regiment* itself, and by far the longest. In brief, although both of his daughters are married, John of Canace continues to share his wealth with them up to the point of impoverishing himself. Facing destitution,

John concocts a ruse in which his daughters see him counting a large sum of money and putting it in a chest. Convinced of his financial stability and hoping to gain access to the box, the daughters take John into their homes and support him until his death. When the chest is opened, it is empty save for a serjeant's mace bearing a monitory exhortation.

Many critics weigh in with interpretations of the John of Canace story because of its position in the text, its length, and the fact that Hoccleve makes his direct plea to Henry for money following this *exemplum*. Strohm emphasizes the constructed nature of authority in this tale, which "is undeniably shrewd, but also cynical, in its perception that even an empty or vacuous center of authority can constitute subjects as good citizens so long as it engages their desires."[127] For Perkins, the tale speaks to Hoccleve's preoccupation with the process of interpretation, and the exchange of words for money. Hoccleve revises de Cessolis' text warning against financial foolishness into one about "rulers [who] cannot afford to ignore the welfare of their people."[128] Scanlon also weighs in on the John of Canace *exemplum*, seeing it as demonstrating the interdependence of subjects and the royal prerogative, "demonstrating kingship's dependence on its own ideology and those, like Hoccleve, who maintain that ideology."[129] John recognizes that his position as patriarch is constructed, and is thus able to manipulate his daughters into continuing to care for him despite his personal poverty. Importantly, Scanlon argues that Hoccleve expects both Henry and his audience, the "nobility and urban patrichiate," to understand that this interdependence works in their favor.[130] As I argue throughout this chapter, Scanlon's point about interdependence is key to understanding the *Regiment*; however, as does Perkins, I must question whether or not this celebrates an absolute monarchy.[131] The fact that the kind of power relations that Hoccleve represents here are constructed, as Strohm asserts, ensures that the monarch's powers are limited, and not absolute as Scanlon claims. Henry and the nobility can understand that they benefit from this set of mutual obligations, but I argue that Hoccleve and other bureaucrats in his audience can understand that bureaucrats gain from it also.[132]

The mace and its inscription demonstrate the limitation on power based in mutual responsibility. When John's daughters finally open the chest, they: "fond right noght / But a passyngly greet sergeantes mace / In which ther gayly maad was and ywroght / This same scripture: 'I, John of Canace, / Make swich testament heere in this place: / Who berith charge of othir men and is / Of hem despyside, slayn be he with this.'"[133] This inscription models how power relations are interdependent elsewhere in this *exemplum*, in the *Regiment* as a whole, and, I argue, more widely throughout late medieval culture. What critics fail to note is its direction at multiple targets; *both* John *and* his daughters have "charge of othir men." Initially, John supports his daughters despite their affluent marriages, and his daughters "despyse" him for his efforts: "they wax unkynde unto him anoon."[134] Later on, John's daughters have charge of John, and clearly he despises them for it: "hir berdes shaved he right smoothe and cleene."[135]

If the message in the box applies equally to John and his daughters, then what does the mace represent? Strohm's opinion deserves to be quoted at length:

> the mace is an emblem of constituted civil authority, and thus sits two-sidedly in the narration, as an admonition to the prince as well as his subjects. To "bear charge," in this case, has an obviously double meaning: not just to pay the costs but to bear responsibility, the latter the province of the prince.[136]

This convincing interpretation fails to carry its reading far enough, however. Both the prince and his subjects have responsibilities; both pay the costs. Scanlon reminds us that a mace was carried by the sergeant of the House of Commons; nevertheless, he considers this mace a reminder of the real power wielded by rulers.[137] I disagree because the parties carrying maces simultaneously benefited from delegated royal power and were confident and successful in defying the king when it suited their own interests, as the Commons and London did frequently in the late fourteenth and fifteenth centuries. The Mayor of London also carried a ceremonial mace, and his prerogative court, the London Mayor's Court, parallels the king's powers in royal noncommon law courts like Council, Chancery, and later Star Chamber. The mace points more toward the limitations on royal power, then, rather than to a reminder of unquestioned royal prerogative. Power relations were complex, not unidirectional, and Henry could be depicted as a strong (future) monarch at the same time he was shown to have obligations to people lower on the social scale.

Hoccleve's plea to Henry for payment of his annuity bears out this interpretation. Directly following the opening of John of Canace's chest, Hoccleve returns to the position he occupied in the Dialogue with the Old Man, a scapegrace not dissimilar to the role of the profligate John. Each man's financial problems can be the same: "he that but lytil hath may doon excesse / In his degree as wel as may the ryche."[138] Just as both John and his daughters might bear charge of other men, so both Hoccleve and Henry may share financial obligations.

But Hoccleve lays out for Henry *why* he has no money, and suddenly it has nothing to do with profligacy, but everything to do with his professional position in royal government: "my yeerly guerdoun, myn annuitee, / That was me grauntid for my long labour, / Is al behynde—I may nat payed be; / Which causith me to lyven in langour."[139] "Guerdoun" reinforces "annuitee," as both bore connotations of reward or recompense, and Hoccleve highlights this again by noting his "long labour."[140] Together the terms begin the stanza by highlighting that Hoccleve has *worked*, just as Caesar's knight has, and that he is *owed* something. In short, whoever "berith charge" of his annuity has not done his job. In the context of the Canace *exemplum* this comment takes on a warning tone. For, as the John of Canace *exemplum* states, "who berith charge of othir men and is / Of hem despysed, slayne be he" with the mace, the symbol of royal power delegated to, and sometimes resisted by, the communities.[141]

The bureaucrat ends by sounding a stern note of warning to his prince with historical references. Hoccleve cautions that "what kyng that dooth more excessyf despenses / Than his land may to souffyse or atteyne / Shal be destroyed," and reminds the prince that people dependant on monies drawn on royal coffers spent their earnings, and had no way to refill their pockets if the royal treasury was empty.[142] Hoccleve suggests that civil unrest might be caused by a kind of breach of contract that occurs when dependents, like himself, go unremunerated for service rendered.

Caesar and his soldier, the king and the fool, John and his daughters each held a responsibility to the other. Subordinates used their expertise for the benefit of rulers, while the rulers were to demonstrate their appreciation for this labor by recognizing their servants in a bureaucratic form of Langland's "right relations." Yet Hoccleve's response to the problem of mixing law and maintenance ethically was not to become general practice until long after Hoccleve and the Lancastrian government were gone. The political uncertainty of the fifteenth century prevented any great leap forward. Nevertheless, both Hoccleve and Gower identified and addressed how maintenance was fundamentally in conflict with impartial practice of the law and both made concrete suggestions about how this tension could be ameliorated.

Ruminating on Retaining

While this book ends with a chapter about legal personnel and "economic ethics," the law as a topic has furnished a throughline from the beginning, and one specially suited to a literary project. After all, law does not always reflect reality: as Fowler no less than Natalie Davis reminds us, the law is full of fictions. But legal fictions, no less than literary fictions, tell us something about a society's desires and hopes, and ethics is certainly an arena for desires and hopes. Legal fictions are, in Burger's words, "good to think with." When lawmen and poets, some of whom were lawmen themselves, suggested analogies between husbands and lords and wives and servants, they were creating fiction. Like any legislation, these analogies, themselves "good to think with," were an attempt to lay down the law on recalcitrant reality. But thanks to the connections between law and literature, thanks to the fact that they are both fiction, to an extent, and some shared authors, the legal analogies can be useful in decoding literature. When applied in this way, these branches of service culture reveal interpretations that I think do not come easily to modern readers.

Accepting and comprehending the late medieval notion of limited and unequal autonomy poses a challenge for modern scholars that may make the relationship between lord and man and husband and wife look less culturally significant than it would have been for a medieval person. Today, we fetishize personal freedom, and clearly, the late medieval English did not. Or perhaps those who wrote laws and literature did not wish to promote unfettered autonomy: they did not desire it, and did not hope for it. For them, such freedom was unethical. In the twenty-first century we must attempt instead to see these unequal relationships through medieval eyes: as both respected and reciprocal. Even so, medieval authors were aware that these unequal relationships could sometimes compromise what they regarded as basic human rights. The relationship between the law and legal personnel provides a final example: when the government could not or would not pay its members more than lords could, lawmen took advantage of the legal system, even knowing that their choices might render the law partial.

In the end, while medieval English service culture was not the Mob, I think the cultural parallels are too important to ignore. Networks of kinship and loyalty surround us still, even if the terms for them are not as good to think with as they once were. The educated, middle class "we" distance ourselves from service networks when we name them "gangs." When we call them family, we embrace them, and they embrace us. We depend upon these matrices, and hope that they do not harm us when we call them the police, or federal, state, or local administration. In turning a blind eye to institutional influence, and a prejudiced one on gangs, we oversimplify social puzzles that have eluded solution for hundreds of years. Activists and others in social service fields work to turn our attention to these issues today, and apply their considerable creativity toward developing solutions. As a medievalist, I turn my gaze on the past, and work to develop a greater understanding of the early development of these fundamental social patterns in our Anglophone culture.

As this book has developed over time, one criticism laid against it has been lack of an endpoint. However, I feel that claiming there was a conclusion to this debate about retaining would be perpetuating a myth we like to tell ourselves: we prefer to believe that these patterns are fully in the past, that this practice's genealogy has no modern members. Yet, even coverture has only quite recently entirely faded from the legal landscape in Britain and the United States. As I admit at the beginning of this book, the notion of service has changed over time. Nevertheless, relations between the descendants of these analogous unequal relationships, lord and retainer, and husband and wife, surround us all. I end, therefore, with "medieval" service. As scholars, we enforce a divider between "medieval" and "Early Modern," and I use it here for its very arbitrariness. I seek to explore a way of organizing society and expressing that organization in analogies, that both protected and harmed late medieval England. While a scholar might prefer a topic that fits a neat teleology, there is none here. Retaining was complicated in the fourteenth century, and it remained no less complicated and no less a part of culture and literature in the fifteenth century. Instead of suggesting simplifications, then, this book has sought to follow the medieval authors whose work forms its focus. This book has attempted to identify and to describe retaining, to explore how it functioned on a personal and institutional level, and to expose other practices with which it conflicted, and with which it was compared. The retinues appearing in Chaucer, Langland, Gower, Hoccleve, and the others provide the opportunity to explore how retaining was illustrated in literature, and how medieval authors struggled themselves to decode its processes. Describing these struggles and attempting to set them into their social context can only help critics read these and other medieval English texts in a more culturally sensitive fashion. To do so is a very postmodern ethic.

NOTES

1 Introducing Medieval Maintenance

1. Lest we believe that a positive perspective on gang activity is impossible, consider that a number of organizations, including the Mob and the Black Panthers, touted the community services they provided. To see "organized crime" as entirely evil may be an expression of American postwar middle-class culture, with its racialized veil of whiteness, rather than an unquestionable moral position.

2. Anthony Musson uses the term "Mafiosi," but does so in arguing against it as an effective analogy in *Public Order and Law Enforcement: The Local Administration of Criminal Justice 1294–1350* (Woodbridge, Suffolk: Boydell Press, 1996), p. 264.

3. Barbara Hanawalt, *Crime and Conflict in English Communities, 1300–1348* (Cambridge: Cambridge University Press, 1979), p. 221. It should be noted that by 1998, she chose to avoid the loaded term "Mafia" and used studies of white-collar crime to coin her own term, "fur-collar crime" for noble criminality in *"Of Good and Ill Repute": Gender and Social Control in Medieval England* (Oxford: Oxford University Press, 1998), especially Chapter 4.

4. British audiences are better off here, benefiting from a culture including a tradition of service. Anyone who wants to see this notion of service and its lack demonstrated might consider different readings of the famous relationship between J.R.R. Tolkien's characters Frodo and Sam in the *Lord of the Rings*. British audiences recognize this relationship as the close one between a traditional (perhaps stereotypical) master and servant. At the same time, lacking a similar tradition of service, this relationship appears to American audiences to be either an especially homosocial friendship or a homosexual couple.

5. Abbot-monk was the other recognized analogy. The gravest proof of the currency of these analogies was the codification of a law of petty treason in the 1352 Statute of Treasons, where a servant killing a master, a wife a husband, or anyone his prelate were all considered traitors: see 5 Stat. EdwIII c. 2. For examples of these relationships

used as analogous, see 14 EdwIII, case 49 where the legal prejudice of a canon is directly related to that of a *femme couvert*: "celuy qest obedient navera jammes accion si il ne soit de corporel trespas fait a luy mesme, et unqore ceo coveynt estre fait ovesqe son sovereyn" [one who is in obedience shall never have an action except in respect of corporal trespasses committed against himself, and even then it must be undertaken with the Head of his House] Alfred J. Harwood, ed. *Year Books of the Reign of King Edward the Third.* (London: His Majesty's Stationary Office, 1896). Similarly, the legal relationship of husband and wife was compared to abbot and monk in L.C. Hecher and Michael Hecher, eds. *Year Books of Richard II. 8–10 Richard II 1385–1387* (London: Ames Foundation, 1987), 8 RII, case 13. For clarification, regnal years are denoted by the year of a king's reign (in the example above, the fourteenth year of Edward III's reign). When convenient, I will identify Year Book cases by case number as well as regnal year, as I do above. Chris Given-Wilson's recent electronic version of the Parliamentary Rolls also includes contemporary statutes: see Chris Given-Wilson, ed. *The Parliament Rolls of Medieval England*, Scholarly Digital Editions 2005, hereafter abbreviated PROME. Statutes, like Year Book cases, will be cited by statute number, regnal year, and chapter when applicable.

6. Elizabeth Fowler, "Civil Death and the Maiden: Agency and the Conditions of Contract in *Piers Plowman*," *Speculum* 70 (1995): 760–92, esp. 768. J.H. Baker also provides a legal introduction to coverture in, *An Introduction to English Legal History*, 4th ed. (London: Butterworths, 2002). Chief Justice Belknap expresses the contemporary perspective when he states that "le baron et la femme sount vn mesme person en ley" [the husband and wife are one and the same person in law] in Isobel Thornley, ed. *Year Books of II Richard II 1387–1388* (London: Spottiswood, Ballantyne, & Co., 1937), 2 RII, case 9. Also consider 19 EdwIII, case 42, where in answer to whether one could charge a husband damages for a tort done by his wife, Justice Willoughby responds succinctly: "Pur quei nient?" [Why not?].

7. Fowler, "Civil Death," p. 768.

8. MED, "maintenaunce." OED, "maintainer," "maintenance." Frances McSparran, chief ed. *The Electronic Middle English Dictionary* (Ann Arbor, MI: University of Michigan Press, 2001), and John Simpson, chief ed. *Oxford English Dictionary* (Oxford: University of Oxford Press, 2007).

9. For one consideration about the importance of friends among gentry networks, see Philippa Maddern, "'Best Trusted Friends': Concepts and Practices of Friendship among Fifteenth-century

Norfolk Gentry," in *England in the Fifteenth Century: Proceedings of the 1992 Harlaxton Symposium*, ed. Nicholas Rogers (Stamford: Paul Watkins, 1994), pp. 100–117.

10. Richard Kaeuper and Philippa Maddern are notable exceptions here, see for example Philippa Maddern, *Violence and the Social Order: East Anglia 1422–1442* (Oxford: Clarendon Press, 1992) and Richard Kaeuper, *War, Justice, and Public Order: England and France in the Later Middle Ages* (Oxford: Oxford University Press, 1988), and both historians have other works in this vein.

11. In the interest of precision, I will generally use the term "autonomy" throughout this book to the more commonly seen "agency." Carolynn Van Dyke asks some provocative questions about literary critics' use of the term agency in *Chaucer's Agents: Cause and Representation in Chaucerian Narrative* (Cranbury, NJ: Fairleigh Dickinson University Press, 2005), pp. 13–26.

12. K.B. McFarlane, *The Nobility of Later Medieval England* (Oxford: Clarendon, 1973), particularly Chapter 1, part vi.

13. McFarlane, *Nobility*, p. 105.

14. For examples of just how complex these networks could be, in McFarlane's view, see *Lancastrian Kings and Lollard Knights* (Oxford: Clarendon, 1972), especially Part Two.

15. McFarlane, *Nobility*, p. 106.

16. McFarlane, *Nobility*, p. 113.

17. Chris Given-Wilson, *The Royal Household and the King's Affinity: Service, Politics and Finance in England, 1360–1413* (New York: Yale University Press, 1986), p. 203. I am especially indebted to chapter 4 in what follows. In addition, I must recognize that the historians quoted here are exemplary samples of a much larger group of historians studying maintenance and retaining.

18. J.M.W. Bean, *From Lord to Patron: Lordship in Late Medieval England* (Manchester: Manchester University Press, 1989), p. 179.

19. Given-Wilson, *Royal Household*, p. 203.

20. Christine Carpenter, *Locality and Polity: A Study of Warwickshire Landed Society, 1401–1499* (Cambridge: Cambridge University Press, 1992), pp. 335–36.

21. Bean, *Lord*, p. 236.

22. Simon Walker, *The Lancastrian Affinity, 1361–1399* (Oxford: Clarendon, 1990), p. 1.

23. Walker, *Lancastrian*, p. 17.

24. Walker, *Lancastrian*, p. 84.

25. Bean, *Lord*, p. 236.

26. Walker, *Lancastrian*, p. 16.

27. Michael Hicks, *Bastard Feudalism* (New York: Longman, 1995), p. 8.

28. Walker, *Lancastrian*, p. 103.

29. Walker, *Lancastrian*, p. 261.

30. McFarlane, *Nobility*, p. 115.

31. Hicks, *Bastard*, p. 120.

32. J.G. Bellamy, *Crime and Public Order in England in the Later Middle Ages* (London: Routledge, 1973), pp. 21–22.

33. J.G. Bellamy, *Bastard Feudalism and the Law* (Portland, OR: Aeropagitica Press, 1989), p. 80.

34. For example, see Bellamy, *Bastard Feudalism*, pp. 28, 66.

35. Bellamy, *Bastard Feudalism*, p. 95.

36. Bellamy, *Bastard Feudalism*, p. 96.

37. Musson, *Public Order*, p. 1. Musson also discusses this development in his newer book, *Medieval Law in Context: The Growth of Legal Consciousness from Magna Carta to the Peasants' Revolt* (Manchester: Manchester University Press, 2001), particularly Chapter 1.

38. David Gary Shaw, *Necessary Conjunctions: The Social Self in Medieval England* (New York: Palgrave, 2005) and Raluca Radulescu, *The Gentry Context for Malory's* Morte Darthur (Cambridge: D.S. Brewer, 2003).

2   Maintaining a Family

1. Christine Carpenter, ed. *Kingsford's Stonor Letters and Papers 1290–1483* (Cambridge: Cambridge University Press, 1996), p. 17.

2. For general information on the Stonors, see also Christine Carpenter, "The Stonor Circle in the Fifteenth Century," in *Rulers and Ruled in Late Medieval England*, ed. Rowena Archer and Simon Walker (London: Hambledon Press, 1995), p. 25 [175–200]. For information on Judge Stonor, see P.J. Jefferies, "Profitable Fourteenth-Century Legal Practice and Landed Investment: The Case of Judge Stonor, c. 1281–1354," *Southern History* 15 (1993): 18–33.

3. For general history of the family, see Joan Kirby, "A Fifteenth-Century Family, The Plumptons of Plumpton, and Their Lawyers, 1461–1515," *Northern History* 25 (1989): 106–119. For a minute analysis of local gentry families and their relationships with the Plumptons around mid-century, see Ruth Wilcock, "Local Disorder in the Honour of Knaresborough, c. 1438–1461 and the National Context," *Northern History* 41 (2004): 39–80.

4. Colin Richmond gives an example that should make us pause before assuming gentry clannishness was without its complexity: he details a thorough disinheritance by Henry Inglose through the first section

of Chapter 2 in *The Paston Family in the Fifteenth Century: The First Phase* (Cambridge: Cambridge University Press, 1990).

5. Wilcock, "Local Disorder," p. 70.

6. For the legal background of this situation, I am drawing on Colin Richmond, "Elizabeth Clere: Friend of the Pastons," in *Medieval Women: Texts and Contexts in Late Medieval Britain: Essays for Felicity Riddy*, ed. Jocelyn Wogan-Browne, Rosalynn Voaden, Arlyn Diamond, Ann Hutchison, Carol Meale, and Lesley Johnson (Turnhout, Belgium: Brepols, 2000), pp. 251–73.

7. I cite from the letters using the volume, number of the letter, and line number when appropriate. Norman Davis, ed. *Paston Letters and Papers of the Fifteenth Century*, 2 vols. (Oxford: Clarendon, 1971). II. 592–94, 597, 600.

8. Richmond assumes that Clere refers to Easter Day when she gives the day as "Eastern Even", but the MED illustrates uses of "even" meaning "vigil" or "day before," and given the petitionary context of the event, and the penitential nature of the days leading up to Easter, Easter Vigil seems a better candidate (MED, "even").

9. II. 600. 26–27.

10. II. 600. 14–15.

11. II. 600. 2–3.

12. II. 600. 7–8.

13. II. 600. 8–10.

14. II. 600. 11–13.

15. For a recent extended treatment of the importance of reputation, or "worship," among the gentry, see Radulescu, *The Gentry Context*, especially Chapter 1.

16. II. 600. 18–19.

17. II. 600. 25–26.

18. II. 600. 29.

19. II. 600. 1, 47, 52.

20. II. 600. 41–42.

21. MED, "double."

22. II. 580. 19–20.

23. I. 185. 42–43, I. 38, 52, 59, 133, for example.

24. II. 600. 48.

25. II. 600. 36–37.

26. Carole Rawcliffe and Susan Flower, "English Noblemen and Their Advisers: Consultation and Collaboration in the Later Middle Ages," *Journal of British Studies* 25 (1986): 157–77.

27. II. 594. 2.

28. II. 594. 4–5.

29. The first attested use of "appointement" is 1417, and most first uses date to mid-century; Lord Scales was being up-to-date with his vocabulary. MED, "appointement."
30. II. 594. 1.
31. II. 594. 5–6.
32. Walker, *Lancastrian*, 9.
33. See Richmond, "Clere," p. 255, for a discussion of this phenomenon.
34. II. 592. 3.
35. II. 593. 3.
36. Carpenter, *Kingsford*. Until the fifteenth century, the letters are in Anglo-French, and although fascinating and deserving study in their own right, to provide overlap with the Paston and Plumpton letters, I have selected examples from the Middle English correspondence here. Letters will be cited by letter number.
37. Carpenter, "Stonor Circle," p. 195.
38. Letter 63.
39. Letter 63.
40. For the concept of honor and shame among the gentry as distinct from that of the nobility, see Philippa Maddern, "Honour Among the Pastons: Gender and Integrity in Fifteenth-Century English Provincial Society," *Journal of Medieval History* 14 (1988): 357–71.
41. Letter 64.
42. Letter 64.
43. Kingsford gives this information in his introduction to his edition of the letters; however he does not give more detailed citations.
44. Letter 69. For their relationship, see Carpenter, "Stonor Circle," p. 184.
45. Letter 69.
46. Letter 81.
47. Letter 81.
48. Letter 81.
49. Letter 79.
50. Letter 79.
51. Letter 79.
52. Letter 80.
53. Letter 80.
54. The last we hear of the dispute in the letters is in 91, dated October 8, 1468, where Thomas Stonor reports to his wife Jane that "I thanke God myne adversari of Devonshere hathe had no wurshyp:....he is shamyd and nonsuyd in the cort to his great shame." The lawsuits finally found an end, with a jury dismissing the case.
55. A brief but powerful additional example of a man calling upon his lords for aid is John Chancy. Describing himself as a squire

of the Duke of Exeter, Chancy entered into a disputed property, and to ensure its continued possession by his family, enfeoffed the Duke of Exeter, the Duke of Buckingham, and the Earl of Eu in it. We know about the event from the rival claimant's letters and petition to Parliament for redress against such powerful opponents. See pages 177–78 and 191–92 in Christine Carpenter, ed. *The Armburgh Papers: The Brokholes Inheritance in Warwickshire, Hertfordshire, and Essex c.1417–1453* (Woodbridge, Suffolk: The Boydell Press, 1998).

56. Thomas Stapleton, ed. *The Plumpton Correspondence* (Gloucester: Alan Sutton, 1990). Letters will be cited by letter number. Letter 1.
57. Letter 17.
58. Letter 17.
59. Wilcock refers frequently to Mauleverer's Neville association. See, for example, "Local Disorder," p. 60.
60. Letter 15.
61. Letter 15.
62. Letter 2.
63. Letter 4.
64. See note h to Letter 6.
65. Letter 6.
66. Letter 9.
67. This new link was not to succeed, however, as by the late 1460s, Plumpton was harassed by the York see for his immoral living with Joan Wintringham. (The Archbishop at the time, it should be noted, was a Neville.) In 1468, Plumpton finally recognized her as his legal wife, and found witnesses to pledge that the clandestine marriage dated to the 1450s. This made their child Robert William's legal heir, and threw into question the settlements of each granddaughter, including the Roucliffe. In the end it was this hedging of Plumpton's bets that landed Robert in court in repeated attempts to gain control of his inheritance.

3   Attaining Women

1. See p. 3 in chapter 1 above.
2. For a pointed example, see Susan Crane's reading of the *Franklin's Tale* that identifies Dorigen's struggles with the class struggles of franklins: "The Franklin as Dorigen," *Chaucer Review* 24 (1990): 236–52. In general, see David Aers and Lynn Staley, *Powers of the Holy: Religion, Politics, and Gender in Late Medieval English Culture* (University Park, PA: Pennsylvania State Press, 1996).

3. This phrase is used by Glenn Burger in *Chaucer's Queer Nation* (Minneapolis, MN: University of Minnesota Press, 2003), p. 44, where he argues that the conjugal pair was "good to think with" for the medieval English for different reasons than I do here. Recently, Matthew Giancarlo has argued that parliament, too, was "good to think with" in the late fourteenth century, and he also links parliament with marriage. It seems that marriage was truly "good to think with." Matthew Giancarlo, *Parliament and Literature in Late Medieval England* (Cambridge: Cambridge University Press, 2007), p. 138.

4. All Chaucer citations will be to the Riverside edition, using Benson's abbreviations for work title and line number. Larry Benson, ed. *The Riverside Chaucer*, 3rd ed. (Boston: Houghton Mifflin, 1987). Tr, V, 825.

5. Burger, *Queer Nation*, p. 46, 58. Cultural diglossia seems implicit in Burger's use of cultural hybridity, and I think the term nicely captures the cultural matrix in which the authors and characters I study find themselves. Criseyde, Dorigen, John Paston, and Thomas Hoccleve speak multiple languages of power and submission, and adeptly code-switch when the occasion demands.

6. In addition, the example of 19 EdwIII, case 24 demonstrates that a wife could not legally be considered part of the same conspiracy her husband took part in, "pur ceo qe tut serreit acompte le fait le baron" ["the whole would be accounted the act of the husband"].

7. I will discuss attempts to control retinues through legislation further in chapter 4.

8. For excellent discussions of the complexities of the medieval English definition of *raptus*, see Christopher Cannon, "Chaucer and Rape: Uncertainty's Certainties," in *Representing Rape in Medieval and Early Modern Literature*, ed. Elizabeth Robertson and Christine Rose (New York: Palgrave), pp. 255–79; Henry Ansgar Kelly, "Meanings and Uses of *Raptus* in Chaucer's Time," *Studies in the Age of Chaucer* 20 (1998): 101–65; and Corinne Saunders, *Rape and Ravishment in the Literature of the Middle Ages* (Cambridge: D.S. Brewer, 2001).

9. Rape remains fraught in courtrooms today, where the legal boundaries of both "forced" and "coitus" are under debate. Cases exploring so-called gray rape are good examples of the perpetual attempts to fix a legal definition.

10. Christine Rose voices an all-too common approach to the problem when she wants to recover the body of the raped woman in Chaucer's texts; "Chaucer's audience discovers indeed that the

rapes in his narratives are tropes for decidedly alternative purposes than highlighting violence to women," and later "women...must read to recover the literal sense of the trope," p. 22. As a feminist, I applaud Rose's and similar critics' awareness of how our own female bodies color our readings of Chaucer's texts. However, I seek in this chapter a more culturally embedded way to read medieval narratives of rape. Christine Rose, "Reading Chaucer Reading Rape," in *Representing Rape in Medieval and Early Modern Literature*, ed. Elizabeth Robertson and Christine Rose (New York: Palgrave, 2001), pp. 21–60.

11. 1 Stat. 6 RII c. 6. The second Statute of Westminster (1 Stat. 13 EdwI c. 34) identified rape as a felony whether or not the woman consented before or after the event.

12. Even more fascinating, this statute did not end appeals in practice. Christopher Cannon illustrates instances of appeal of what we would today consider rape dating to after the statute; "*Raptus* in the Chaumpaigne Release and a Newly Discovered Document Concerning the Life of Geoffrey Chaucer," *Speculum* 68 (1993): 74–94. In a very positive interpretation of the slippery nature of the law of rape, Sue Sheridan Walker suggests that "the common law concerning domestic relations permitted the self-will of an unhappily married woman in leaving her husband to be played out in the guise of an abduction.... The husbands of 'abducted' wives could secure only damages usually equivalent to the value of chattels 'taken' with his wife but never recover her person," in "The Feudal Family and the Common Law Courts: The Pleas Protecting Rights of Wardship and Marriage, c. 1225–1375," *Journal of Medieval History* 14 (1988): 13–31, esp. 24. For contemporary debate, see Samuel Thorne, ed. *Yearbooks of Richard II. 6 Richard II 1382–1383* (London: Ames Foundation, 1996), 6 RII, case 20, where Justice Skipwith argues that the word "rapuit" sounds in felony, just as the theft of a horse would; according to him, only a wife "abducta" could be prosecuted as a civil offense.

13. Elizabeth Robertson notes that study of medieval marriage and rape "[has] implications for our understanding of medieval subjectivity and agency." My own examination of this pairing travels a different path than Robertson's; however, her recognition of the usefulness of such study argues that we might all pay greater attention to these topics. Elizabeth Robertson, " 'Raptus' and the Poetics of Married Love in Chaucer's Wife of Bath's Tale and James I's *Kingis Quair*," in *Reading Medieval Culture: Essays in Honor of Robert W. Hanning*, ed. Robert M. Stein and Sandra Pierson

Prior (Notre Dame, IN: University of Notre Dame Press, 2005), pp. 302–23, esp. 303.

14. H. Marshall Leicester, "'My Bed Was Ful of Verray Blood': Subject, Dream, and Rape in the Wife of Bath's Prologue and Tale," in *Geoffrey Chaucer: The Wife of Bath*, ed. Peter Beidler (Boston: St. Martin's Press, 1996), pp. 235–54. Cannon notices the same distinction between statute law and the common law.

15. Cannon, *Raptus*: 80–81, for example. For an entire monograph devoted to the topic of the culture of common law and how it related to the statutary law, see J.W. Tubbs, *The Common Law Mind: Medieval and Early Modern Conceptions* (Baltimore: Johns Hopkins University Press, 2000).

16. Leicester, "Verray Blood," pp. 246–47.

17. "Medieval marriage law" was overwhelmingly canon law, of course, in England as elsewhere. As my special interest is in maintenance, however, and as I am examining the ways in which husbands and wives were seen as analogous to pairs of men in the common law, I am concentrating on common law relevant to marriage.

18. Leicester, "Verray Blood," pp. 247–48.

19. Critics have tapped nearly every long work of Chaucer's as exploring the issue of rape in some way. This chapter constitutes a survey then, that I believe is at once representative and noncontentious in its selection of assaults. I have chosen texts pertinent to the larger theme of the book, and at the same time texts that enabled me to write a chapter approximately the same length as the others, and not a book unto itself. To that end, a number of related instances are not discussed here, such as Philomela in the *Legend of Good Women*, the *Man of Law's Tale*, and the *Clerk's Tale*, to name just a few.

20. FranT, 1474.

21. FranT, 1622.

22. A number of critics will be discussed below, but see the following for a sampling of recent contributions in this area: Burger, *Queer Nation*, pp. 113–18 (examines the false autonomy Dorigen is supposed to enjoy); David Raybin, "'Wommen, of Kynde, Desiren Libertee': Rereading Dorigen, Rereading Marriage," *Chaucer Review* 27 (1992): 65–86 (considers Dorigen as the motive force of the narrative); Elizabeth Robertson, "Marriage, Mutual Consent, and the Affirmation of the Female Subject in the *Knight's Tale*, the *Wife of Bath's Tale*, and the *Franklin's Tale*," in *Drama, Narrative, and Poetry in the Canterbury Tales*, ed. Wendy Harding (Toulouse, France: Publications Universitaire de Mirail, 2003), pp. 175–93 (considers the agency of Dorigen and Arveragus as heavily

influenced by the theological insistence on consent in marriage); and Mark N. Taylor, "Servant and Lord/ Lady and Wife: The *Franklin's Tale* and Traditions of Courtly and Conjugal Love," *Chaucer Review* 32 (1997): 64–81 (relates the FranT to Chrétien de Troyes' companionate couples).

23. Andrea Rossi-Reder, "Male Movement and Female Fixity in the *Franklin's Tale* and *Il Filocolo*," in *Masculinities in Chaucer: Approaches to Maleness in the* Canterbury Tales *and* Troilus and Criseyde, ed. Peter Beidler (Cambridge: D.S. Brewer, 1998), pp. 105–16, esp. 115.

24. Saunders, *Rape and Ravishment*, p. 294.

25. Carolynn Van Dyke, "The Clerk's and the Franklin's Subjected Subjects," *Studies in the Age of Chaucer* 17 (1995): 45–68.

26. Van Dyke, "Subjected Subjects": 51.

27. Van Dyke, "Subjected Subjects": 60.

28. Van Dyke, "Subjected Subjects": 63. Without direct recourse to the topic of coverture, Burger also sees Dorigen's ultimate constraint as necessary for the reproduction of the developing conjugal culture characteristic of the fourteenth-century middle class: Burger, *Queer Nation*, pp. 117–18.

29. Van Dyke, "Subjected Subjects": 65.

30. Richard Firth Green, "Chaucer's Victimized Women," *Studies in the Age of Chaucer* 10 (1988): 3–21.

31. Richard Firth Green, *A Crisis of Truth: Literature and Law in Ricardian England* (Philadelphia: University of Pennsylvania Press, 1999).

32. Green, *Crisis*, p. 334.

33. Francine McGregor, "What of Dorigen? Agency and Ambivalence in the *Franklin's Tale*," *Chaucer Review* 31 (1997): 365–78.

34. McGregor, "Agency and Ambivalence": 367.

35. McGregor, "Agency and Ambivalence": 369.

36. McGregor, "Agency and Ambivalence": 373.

37. FranT, 745–48, 751–52.

38. Rowena Archer, " 'How Ladies...Who Live on Their Manors ought to Manage Their Households and Estates' Women as Landholders and Administrators in the Later Middle Ages," in *Women in English Society c. 1200–1500*, ed. P.J.P. Goldberg (Stroud, Gloucestershire: Alan Sutton, 1992), pp. 149–81. Wives could formally act as their husband's attorneys in court, too; see 8 EdwIII, case 11.

39. FranT, 995–97.

40. FranT, 1341–45.

41. FranT, 1351.

42. FranT, 1362–63.

43. John M. Fyler includes a very nice breakdown and discussion of the lament in "Love and Degree in the *Franklin's Tale*," *Chaucer Review* 21 (1987): 321–37.

44. FranT, 1422–23.

45. For a different perspective on Dorigen's agency, one identifying male agency as practiced in public, and therefore apparently more effective than women's agency, practiced in private, and therefore less apparent, see Andrea Rossi-Reder, "Female Fixity."

46. FranT, 1474.

47. FranT, 1479, emphasis mine.

48. FranT, 1543–44.

49. Isabelle Mast presents the exception that proves the rule. She manages to "uncover the woman" in Gower's rape accounts in both the *Confessio Amantis* and the *Mirour de l'homme* while keeping them within some historical context: "Rape in John Gower's *Confessio Amantis* and Other Related Works," in *Young Medieval Women*, ed. Katherine J. Lewis, Noël J. Menuge, and Kim Phillips (New York: St. Martin's Press, 1999), pp. 103–32.

50. Craig Bertholet, "From Revenge to Reform: The Changing Face of 'Lucrece' and Its Meaning in Gower's *Confessio Amantis*," *Philological Quarterly* 70 (1991): 403–21.

51. A good example is Louise Sylvester, who limits her article to the Lucretia stories appearing "in three medieval story-collections: Chaucer's poem *The Legend of Good Women*, Gower's *Confessio Amantis* and Christine de Pizan's story collection *Le Livre de la Cité des Dames*" (p. 115), omitting Lydgate entirely from consideration. Louise Sylvester, "Reading Narratives of Rape: The Story of Lucretia in Chaucer, Gower, and Christine de Pizan," *Leeds Studies in English* 31 (2000): 115–44. For excellent discussion of Lydgate's addition to the corpus, see Saunders, *Rape and Ravishment*, pp. 166–72 and Nigel Mortimer, *John Lydgate's* Fall of Princes *Narrative Tragedy in its Literary and Political Contexts* (Oxford: Clarendon, 2005), especially pp. 61–79.

52. *Legend of Good Women* (hereinafter LGW), 1772, and *Wife of Bath's Tale* (hereinafter WBT), 887.

53. LGW, 1781.

54. I will use Macaulay's edition of *Confessio Amantis*, and cite book and line number. G.C. Macaulay, ed. *The Complete Works of John Gower*, 4 vols. (Oxford: Clarendon Press, 1902), CA, VII, 4894.

55. Textual citations for *Fall of Princes* are from Henry Bergen's edition and cite short title, book, and line numbers. Henry Bergen, ed. *Lydgate's Fall of Princes*, 4 vols. (Oxford: Oxford University Press, 1967).

56. LGW, 1790.
57. CA, VII, 4981.
58. LGW, 1814.
59. *Fall*, II, 1032.
60. Richard Ireland, "Lucrece, Philomela (and Cecily): Chaucer and the Law of Rape," in *Crime and Punishment in the Middle Ages*, ed. Timothy Haskett (Victoria: University of Victoria, 1998), pp. 37–61.
61. Ireland, "Law of Rape," p. 56.
62. Elizabeth Robertson, "Public Bodies and Psychic Domains: Rape, Consent, and Female Subjectivity in Geoffrey Chaucer's *Troilus and Criseyde*," in *Representing Rape in Medieval and Early Modern Literature*, ed. Elizabeth Robertson and Christine Rose (New York: Palgrave, 2001), pp. 282–310, esp. 285.
63. LGW, 1827–28, 1844–47.
64. CA, VII, 5019–20.
65. CA, VII, 5063–64.
66. *Fall*, II, 1039–42, emphasis mine.
67. CA, VII, 5078–79.
68. CA, VII, 5088–90. Others have read this "dedlich" to suggest that Lucretia is in fact dead here, while I assume she is dying. The conditional meaning of the -lich ending suggests that an interpretation is required. Is someone who is "deadlike" alive or dead? Of course, assessing a state of death was hardly scientific in the premodern world: Lear's hope in that feather was a hope shared by many sane people. Here we have a reminder that if a man chooses to act, the woman's actual intentions matter little. Perhaps yet alive, here Lucretia's civil death is personified.
69. LGW, 1680–83, 1861–73.
70. LGW, 1869–70. Most critics consider Chaucer's mentions of the political ramifications of Lucretia's rape to be passing in nature. While I do not mean to argue that Chaucer had a political agenda in the *Legend of Good Women*'s tale of Lucretia, I think that the political angle, included even here, demonstrates well how political the story in general was understood to be.
71. *Fall*, II, 1336–40, see also III, 937–38, III, 960–66.
72. *Fall*, III, 1014–15.
73. *Fall*, III, 1029.
74. *Fall*, III, 1009–11.
75. *Fall*, III, 1018–20.
76. See extended discussions in both Christopher Cannon, "*Raptus*," and Kelly, "Meanings and Uses."
77. *Fall*, III, 1023–27.
78. See MED, "yolden," 1b, c.

79. See for example, "parcial causes in sooth ther may non be/ Atwen vs tweyne," "entirmedle all thynge that is in doubte," and "toward vs bothe the quarell doth rebounde" (*Fall*, III, 1030–31, 1035, 1047).

80. *Fall*, III, 1041–42, emphasis mine.

81. *Fall*, III, 1049–50.

82. *Fall*, III, 1051–57.

83. Of course, we might also recall the *Roman de la Rose* and other texts where a woman's chastity is figured as a besieged castle.

84. *Fall*, III, 1092.

85. *Fall*, III, 1093–94.

86. *Fall*, III, 1065, 1069.

87. *Fall*, III, 1074–56.

88. For information on Chancery, see Margaret Avery, "The History of the Equitable Jurisdiction of Chancery before 1460," *Bulletin of the Institute for Historical Research* 42 (1969): 129–44; Ed. William Baildon, *Select Cases in Chancery A.D.1364–1471*, Seldon Society 10 (London: Seldon Society, 1896); Mark Beilby, "The Profits of Expertise: The Rise of the Civil Lawyers and Chancery Equity," in *Profit, Piety, and the Professions in Later Medieval England*, ed. Michael Hicks (Gloucester: Alan Sutton, 1990), pp. 72–90; Timothy S. Haskett, "Conscience, Justice, and Authority in the Late-Medieval English Court of Chancery," in *Expectations of the Law in the Middle Ages*, ed. Anthony Musson (Woodbridge, Suffolk: Boydell Press, 2001), pp. 151–63; P. Tucker, "The Early History of the Court of Chancery: A Comparative Study," *English Historical Review* 115 (2000): 791–811.

89. *Fall*, III, 1116–20.

90. *Fall*, III, 1133–36, 1128–30.

91. *Fall*, III, 1142–43.

92. Colin Fewer, "John Lydgate's *Troy Book* and the Ideology of Prudence," *Chaucer Review* 38 (2004): 229–45, esp. 236. Given how important the Troy story was to medieval literature, there is surprisingly little critical examination of it, and especially the figure of Helen within that tradition. C. David Benson, *The History of Troy in Middle English Literature* (Woodbridge, Suffolk: D.S. Brewer, 1980), remains the single full-length study.

93. Saunders, *Rape and Ravishment*, p. 178.

94. All citations to the *Troy Book* will include book and line numbers. Henry Bergen, ed. *Lydgate's Troy Book, A. D. 1412–20* (London: Early English Texts Society, 1906–1935).

95. Benson, *History of Troy*, p. 97.

96. All citations to the Laud *Troy Book* will be to J. Ernst Wulfing, ed. *The Laud Troy Book* (Millwood, NY: Early English Text Society, Kraus Reprint, 1988), and cite line numbers.

97. Chaucer makes little mention of Helen in the other major Middle English Troy-text, *Troilus and Criseyde*. For a perspective arguing that Helen's presence nevertheless shapes that text, see Christopher Baswell and Paul Beekman Taylor, "The *Faire Queene Eleyne* in Chaucer's *Troilus*," *Speculum* 63 (1988): 293–311.

98. CA, V, 7213–19.

99. CA, V, 7436–40.

100. *Troy*, I, 4355–63.

101. Laud, 1715–21, 1728. Benson gives the Laud-poet's careful integration of the Hesione incident as an example of the poet's interest in providing a complete history (p. 93).

102. Laud, 1741–42, and 1957. Baswell and Taylor note that Chaucer may be following this tradition in implying that Helen is a whore (p. 306).

103. *Raptus* of virgins was so tightly linked to ravishment of wards that the two can be nearly interchangeable. On wardship see n. 116 in chapter 4.

104. Cannon, "Certainties," p. 264.

105. CA, V, 7515–18.

106. *Troy*, II, 3700–3705, II, 3725, II, 3739–42.

107. *Troy*, II, 3832–39.

108. Laud, 2800, 2808.

109. *Troy*, IV, 1049–75. Benson mentions this scene as an example of Lydgate's dedication to attempting to create a whole historical civilization for his narrative, complete with noncontemporary legal system (p. 110).

110. *Troy*, II, 3901–04, 3912–13. The Laud book's version of this is much shortened; Helen "made moche mone" that she was separated from all she'd previously known, but there is little more discussion of the matter (Laud, 2930).

111. *Troy*, II, 3959–62.

112. *Troy*, II, 4060, 4069–70.

113. WBT, 1224.

114. Gerald Richman, "Rape and Desire in *The Wife of Bath's Tale*," *Studia Neophilologica* 61 (1989): 161–65.

115. Robert J. Blanch, "'Al Was this Land Fulfild of Fayereye': The Thematic Employment of Force, Willfulness, and Legal Conventions in Chaucer's *Wife of Bath's Tale*," *Studia Neophilologica* 57 (1985): 41–51, esp. 41.

116. For example, see T.L. Burton's statement: "the single couplet devoted to the rape itself (887–88) is a masterpiece of compressed dramatic characterization," in "The Wife of Bath's Fourth and Fifth Husbands and Her Ideal Sixth: The Growth of a Marital Philosophy," *Chaucer Review* 13 (1979): 34–50, esp. 45; Elaine Tuttle Hansen, "'Of His Love Daungerous to Me': Liberation, Subversion, and Domestic Violence in the *Wife of Bath's Prologue* and *Tale*," in *Geoffrey Chaucer: The Wife of Bath*, ed. Peter Beidler (Boston: Bedford, 1996), pp. 273–89, 280; Carole Koepke Brown gives an interesting close reading on p. 22, in "Episodic Patterns and the Perpetrator: The Structure and Meaning of Chaucer's *Wife of Bath's Tale*," *Chaucer Review* 31 (1996): 18–35.

117. WBT, 887–88.

118. WBT, 889–90.

119. WBT, 891–93. The Wife adds "paraventure swich was the statut tho" to this passage, however, and Leicester uses the ambiguity inherent in the term to ask questions about the relationship between the crime of rape and marriage (WBT, 893, Leicester, "Verray Blood," pp. 245–47). Hansen also reads this line to suggest that the audience would be unsure of legal penalties for rape (p. 281). I would like to further point out that the Wife's lack of precision about what constituted statute law is echoed in the many examples of rape cases that were prosecuted counter to statute, as discovered by Cannon and Kelly.

120. See the selected examples in the following: Blanch touches on it from the angle of contract law (p. 46); Richman (p. 161), also Biebel (p. 74), in Elizabeth Biebel, "A Wife, a Batterer, and a Rapist: Representations of 'Masculinity' in the *Wife of Bath's Prologue* and *Tale*," in *Masculinities in Chaucer: Approaches to Maleness in the* Canterbury Tales *and* Troilus and Criseyde, ed. Peter Beidler (Cambridge: D.S. Brewer, 1998), pp. 63–75; Brown "Episodic Patterns," p. 21, Robertson, "Poetics," p. 308 Saunders, *Rape and Ravishment*, p. 305.

121. WBT, 1061.

122. WBT, 1070–71.

123. WBT, 1231–32.

124. Consider again the Yearbook case cited earlier where the answer to whether a husband could be prosecuted for his wife's offense was "why not?"

125. WBT, 1243–44, 1255–56.

126. Citations will be to the following edition: Thomas Hahn, ed. *Sir Gawain: Eleven Romances and Tales* (Kalamazoo, MI: Medieval

Institute Publications, 1995). References will be to title and line number.

127. *Sir Gawain*, 629–31.
128. *Sir Gawain*, 635.
129. *Sir Gawain*, 638–40.
130. *Sir Gawain*, 342–53.
131. For a consideration of Arthur's humility here, see Robert Shenk, "The Liberation of the 'Loathly Lady' of Medieval Romance," *Journal of the Rocky Mountain Medieval and Renaissance Association* 2 (1981): 69–77.

4   Retaining Men

1. I explicate the assault as a passage translated with an English audience in mind, and demonstrating an understanding of English legal idiom, in "Maintaining Love Through Accord in the *Tale of Melibee*," *Chaucer Review* 39 (2004): 165–76.
2. This partiality of counsel is not taken into account in Ann Dobyns' exploration of counsel in *Melibee* as a Thomistic practice in "Chaucer and the Rhetoric of Justice," *Disputatio* 4 (1999): 75–89. As do most critics, Judith Ferster ignores the council, to concentrate on Prudence as a counselor, in *Fictions of Advice. The Literature of Counsel in Late Medieval England* (Philadelphia: University of Pennsylvania Press, 1996). Lynn Staley implies the partiality of the council, but also concentrates on Prudence in "Inverse Counsel: Contexts for the *Melibee*," *Studies in Philology* 87 (1990): 137–55. Similarly, David Wallace only implies the council's bias before moving onto Prudence's counsel in Chapter 8 of *Chaucerian Polity: Absolutist Lineages and Associational Forms in England and Italy* (Stanford, CA: Stanford University Press, 1997). Giancarlo concentrates on the council as an example of a parliament, but his interest in the allegory leads his discussion to focus on Prudence, *Parliament*, pp. 148–51.
3. Mel, 1003–6. Recall that references to *Melibee* will be to the Riverside edition, citing fragment, abbreviated title, and line number.
4. For example, Mel, 1554, 1149–52.
5. Mel, 1367. In contrast, the blood ties linking Melibee's enemies to their followers is emphasized: this group of three can together front a large group of "children, bretheren, cosyns, and oother ny kyndrede" (Mel, 1370).
6. Mel, 1368.

7. Mel, 1150–52.

8. Mel, 1008.

9. Mel, 1189, emphasis mine.

10. Mel, 1271–72.

11. Mel, 1273–74.

12. Amanda Walling arrives at this point using different evidence in "'In Hir Tellyng Difference': Gender, Authority, and Interpretation in the *Tale of Melibee*," *Chaucer Review* 40 (2005): 163–81, esp. 170. Giancarlo, too, recognizes that constraint is part of the equation in the *Melibee*: "the woman and the assembly hold similar positions in relation to the lord," *Parliament*, p. 149.

13. I develop my argument about *Melibee* being read as an accord in "Maintaining Love through Accord." For more on accords and arbitrations, see Lorraine Attreed, "Arbitration and the Growth of Urban Liberties in Late Medieval England," *Journal of British Studies* 31 (1992): 205–35; Josephine W. Bennett, "The Mediaeval Loveday," *Speculum* 33 (1958): 351–70, is still the best single piece on accords; Michael Clanchy, "Law and Love in the Middle Ages," in *Disputes and Settlements*, ed. John Bossy (Cambridge: Cambridge University Press, 1983), pp. 47–67; Michael Myers, "The Failure of Conflict Resolution and the Limits of Arbitration in King's Lynn 1405–1416," in *Traditions and Transformations in Late Medieval England*, ed. Sharon Michalove and Douglas Biggs (Boston: Brill, 2002), pp. 81–107; Simon J. Payling, "Law and Arbitration in Nottinghamshire 1399–1461," in *People, Politics, and Community in the Later Middle Ages*, ed. Joel Rosenthal and Colin Richmond (New York: St. Martin's Press, 1987), pp. 140–60; Edward Powell, "Arbitration and the Law in England in the Late Middle Ages," *Transactions of the Royal Historical Society*, 5th ser. 33 (1983): 49–67; Carole Rawcliffe, "The Great Lord as Peacekeeper: Arbitration by English Noblemen and Their Councils in the Later Middle Ages," in *Law and Social Change in British History*, ed. J.A. Guy and H.G. Beale (London: Royal Historical Society, 1984), pp. 34–54; "Parliament and the Settlement of Disputes by Arbitration in the late Middle Ages," *Parliamentary History* 9 (1990): 316–42; and "'That Kindliness Should be Cherished More, and Discord Driven Out': The Settlement of Commercial Disputes by Arbitration in Later Medieval England," in *Enterprise and Individuals in Fifteenth-Century England*, ed. Jennifer Kermode (Stroud, Gloucestershire: Alan Sutton, 1991), pp. 99–117; Ian Rowney, "Arbitration in Gentry Disputes of the Later Middle Ages," *History* 67 (1982): 367–74. Rowney is the only incidence I can find of a scholar

noting the *Melibee*'s resemblance to an accord (p. 370), although Dobyns notes its similarity to the Thomistic process of love; David Smith, "Disputes and Settlements in Medieval Wales: The Role of Arbitration," *The English Historical Review* 106 (1991): 835–60; David Tilsey, "Arbitration in Gentry Disputes: The Case of Bucklow Hundred in Cheshire, 1400–1465," in *Courts, Counties, and the Capital in the Later Middle Ages*, ed. Diana E.S. Dunn (New York: St. Martin's Press, 1996), pp. 53–70.

14. Rot. Parl. iii 302a. This nomenclature refers to the *Rotuli Parliamentorum*, volume three, page 302, column a. For the *Rot. Parl.*'s most recent edition, see PROME.

15. Rawcliffe "Parliament," p. 333.

16. See Meyers for detailed discussion of failed arbitrations and why binding agreements were not always reached.

17. Rawcliffe, "Parliament," p. 340.

18. Traditionally this scene is referred to as the "Rat Parliament"; however, "court" might be a better term, as court has connotations on both the national and the local level, whereas parliament restricts interpretation to the national scale. Citations to the three recensions are as follows: George Kane, ed. *Piers Plowman: The A-Version* (London: University of London Press, 1960); Derek Pearsall, ed. *Piers Plowman the C-text*, 1978 (Exeter: University of Exeter Press, 1999); and for the B text, A.V.C. Schmidt, ed. *The Vision of Piers Plowman*, 1995 (London: J.M. Dent, 1998). Citations to the text will appear in parentheses and will denote the recension, book, and line number.

19. A. Prol. 17. The *Piers Plowman* portions of this chapter are based on ideas from Kathleen E. Kennedy, "Retaining Men (and a Retaining Woman) in *Piers Plowman*," 20 (2006): 191–214, and reworded here with Brepols' kind permission. Although we arrived at them independently, Ralph Hanna makes points about Meed's retaining similar to some of my own voiced in the coming pages. See Chapter Six of *London Literature, 1300–1380* (Cambridge: Cambridge University Press, 2005), esp. pp. 264–73.

20. Lees points out that Meed did not have to be female, and therefore in making her so, Langland is setting his text up to deal with her gender (p. 115). Clare Lees, "Gender and Exchange in *Piers Plowman*," in *Class and Gender in Early English Literature*, ed. Britton J. Harwood and Gillian Overing (Bloomington, IN: Indiana University Press, 1994), pp. 112–30.

21. I am in favor of the revisionist chronology supported by Warner and other Langland critics. Traditionally, critics ascribe the A text

to the later 1360s, B to the later 1370s, and C to the later 1380s. Revisionists have moved these dates forward to before 1377, the late 1380s, and 1390, respectively, and Warner goes further in promoting an A, ur-B, C, B release. Lawrence Warner, "The Ur-B of *Piers Plowman* and the Earliest Production of C and B," *Yearbook of Langland Studies* 16 (2002): 3–39. However, in viewing these recensions as works-in-progress, and in viewing social and political ideas as developing over time, I will be less specific here about recension dates, noting only that the parts of the B text I examine here are parts of the ur-B that Warner posits was extant before C.

22. For critics studying Meed's agency, see especially Fowler, "Civil Death" and Stephanie Trigg, "The Traffic in Medieval Women: Alice Perrers, Feminist Criticism and *Piers Plowman*," *Yearbook of Langland Studies* 12 (1998): 5–29. For a recent exploration of Alice Perrers using documentary evidence, see Mark Ormrod, "Who Was Alice Perrers?" *Chaucer Review* 40 (2006): 219–29.

23. Fowler, "Civil Death," p. 770. For more on coverture see n5–6, chapter 1, above.

24. Fowler, "Civil Death," p. 790.

25. If a *femme couvert* committed a felony, of course, she was still personally liable; she was prejudiced by the law only in civil suits.

26. Trigg, "Traffic," pp. 12–13.

27. Trigg implies that the ambiguity surrounding the date of Perrers' marriage worked in her favor: "Alice needed to be single, acting on her own agency when she lent the money....But when it came to her defense against the charges made in 1377, she needed to be married, and therefore disqualified from any agency implied by the charges" (pp. 15–16).

28. PROME II, 329b, Rot. Parl. ii. 329b. The original French of the complete item reads: "Item, fust fait en ce present parlement une certaine ordenance des femmes pursuantz busoignes en courtz nostre seignur le roi, en la forme qe s'ensuit: Por ce qe pleinte est faite au roy qe aucuns femmes ont pursuys en les courtz du roi diverses busoignes et quereles par voie de maintenance, et pur lower et part avoir, quele chose desplest au roi; et le roi defende qe desormes nulle femme le face, et par especial Alice Perers, sur peine de quanqe la dite Alice purra forfaire, et d'estre bannitz hors du roialme." It should be noted that women are not included in statutory regulation of livery and maintenance after this until 1429, in 1 Stat. 8 HVI c. 4.

29. See, for example, my discussion of the case of Walter Sibille in Kennedy "Retaining," pp. 198–99.

30. See for example 1 Stat. 1 RII c. 4, 1 Stat. 1 RII c. 7, 2 Stat. 8 RII c. 2 and parliamentary debate during these years in *The Statutes of the Realm (1225–1713) Printed by Command of His Majesty King George the Third*. (London: G. Eyre and A. Strahan, 1810–12) or PROME.

31. Meed's father's shifting identity also supports my argument: in other recensions, Meed's father is Wrong, or Favel, who has a fickle tongue. In C, Meed's disparagement of Loyalty harms his work among the law courts especially, and I will deal with the influence of maintenance on the law and legal officials in chapter 5.

32. Kennedy, "Retaining," p. 199.

33. B. 2. 46, 73, 72–107. See Anna Baldwin, *The Theme of Government in Piers Plowman* (Cambridge: D.S. Brewer, 1981), for one extended consideration of Meed as lord of a retinue. For more on retainers acting as witnesses to their lords' documents, see Kennedy, "Retaining," p. 200. Variations between recensions are relatively minor considerations here, so generally I will cite the B text only in this section of my argument.

34. B. 2. 54–55.

35. A. 2. 43, B. 2. 58–62, 108–12.

36. B. 2. 58–62. I will explore contemporary debate about these professions' presence in retinues below in chapter 5.

37. A. 2. 146, 125.

38. B. 2. 114, 63–64.

39. B. 2. 193–205. In fact, the king seems to believe that they are felons, as mainprise was an option for felons only, and only felons could be "hange[d] by the hals" as the king desires to do to them (B. 2. 196, 198). Mainprise pertained to suspected felons only; a mainpernor promised that the defendant would appear in court so that the defendant did not have to remain in custody until the next court. More disturbing is the king's insistence that Guile be summarily executed. Langland makes no mention of why, so we might read this as the king acting tyrannically. However, more likely, given Guile's character, he is an outlaw. The only other time when summary judgment (and execution) could happen was when a felon was caught in the act, which does not seem to be the case here.

40. In a Year Book case noted above, n6 chapter 3, the debate centers around an analogous situation concerning a husband and wife rather than a lord and servant. While the husband and his wife are both named in the writ, and only the wife could be taken into custody, the legal question under discussion was whether to allow

either mainprise if both could be attached. In the end, agreement is reached that neither should be allowed freedom, but Belknap's final note illustrates how seriously issues such union of person were taken, even though they might to us appear academic: "quere tamen qar le contrarie ad este faite souvent" [but yet the contrary is often done], 19 EdwIII, case 24.

41. B. 3. 13–24, emphasis mine. Judges were prohibited formally from taking retainers, finally, in 1384 (3 Stat. 8 RII c. 3), and notions of how ethical it was for a judge to be retained were changing over the years to which the various recensions of *Piers Plowman* date. Recently J.A. Burrow assumed this transaction represented an outright bribe, "Lady Meed and the Power of Money," *Medium Ævum* 74 (2005): 113–18.

42. J.R. Maddicott, *Law and Lordship: Royal Justices as Retainers in Thirteenth- and Fourteenth-Century England* (Oxford: Past and Present Society, 1978), p. 69, argued for a cessation of judicial retaining by the later fourteenth century. Douglas Biggs is forceful in his assertions that retaining continued to play a large role in the bureaucratic and legal professions through the fifteenth century. See his "A Plantagenet Revolution in Government? The Officers of Central Government and the Lancastrian Usurpation of 1399," *Medieval Prosopography* 20 (1999): 191–212 and "Henry IV and His JP's: The Lancastrianization of Justice, 1399–1413," in *Traditions and Transformations in Fifteenth Century England,* ed. Sharon Michalove and Douglas Biggs (Boston: Brill, 2002), pp. 59–79, and most recently *Three Armies in Britain: The Irish Campaign of Richard II and the Usurpation of Henry IV, 1397–99* (Leiden: Brill, 2007), where he emphasizes the importance of these retainers in his conclusion, pp. 273–77 especially.

43. See Kennedy "Retaining," pp. 202–3.

44. A. 3. 83–87.

45. B. 3. 100.

46. Kennedy "Retaining," pp. 203, also see MED, "yeve (n.)."

47. B. 3. 232–33, 238–39, 246, 255–58, C. 3. 304–5.

48. B. 3. 246–47.

49. C. 3. 292; Kennedy "Retaining," p. 204.

50. C. 3. 343, 382–92; Kennedy "Retaining," p. 204.

51. C. 3. 314.

52. C. 3. 382–84.

53. Kennedy "Retaining," p. 205.

54. C. 3. 387–90; Kennedy "Retaining," p. 205.

55. C. 3. 390–92. See MED, "cliaunt"; Kennedy "Retaining," p. 206.

56. The following paragraph is based on five paragraphs in my article "Retaining a Court of Chancery in *Piers Plowman*," *Yearbook of Langland Studies* 17 (2004): 175–89.

57. Here if someone promised to make sure that the malefactor ceased his or her misbehavior, that person stood as a "surety." If money or other valuables such as weapons or jewels were exchanged by the surety (or malefactor) and the wronged party, it was called "waging."

58. B. 4. 94–97; Kennedy "Retaining," p. 207.

59. Traditionally the cat is identified with John of Gaunt and the rodent debate is identified with the Good Parliament as well as the Bad Parliament. For examples, see J.A.W. Bennett, "The Date of the B-Text of *Piers Plowman*," *Medium Ævum* 12 (1943): 55–64. Anna Baldwin and Myra Stokes deserve particular attention in any study of the law and *Piers Plowman*. Baldwin argues that the rodents symbolize a grasping Parliament, and the cat a strict arm of the judicial system. She notes that the collar that the rodents plan to offer the cat resembles livery, but assumes that the collar is the only token of maintenance mentioned in Langland's fable. Anna Baldwin, *The Theme of Government*, pp. 16–18. The historian Helen Jewell rebuts Baldwin's theory thoroughly in "*Piers Plowman*—A Poem of Crisis: An Analysis of Political Instability in Langland's England," in *Politics and Crisis in Fourteenth-Century England*, ed. John Taylor and Wendy Childs (Gloucester: Alan Sutton, 1990), pp. 59–80. In a carefully modulated argument, Myra Stokes sees the rat fable in the B text as the addition of a moral to the traditional point that the rodents are too cowardly to bell the cat: these rodents must also recognize that in a fallen world even a vicious official is better than none. Myra Stokes, *Justice and Mercy in* Piers Plowman. *A Reading of the B Text,* Visio (London: Croom Helm, 1984), especially pages 55–79.

60. Kennedy "Retaining," p. 208. Anne Middleton notes that it was impossible for Langland to truly revise his text, since multiple versions circulated simultaneously in "Acts of Vagrancy: The C Version 'Autobiography' and the Statute of 1388," in *Written Work: Langland, Labor, and Authorship*, ed. Steven Justice and Kathryn Kerby-Fulton (Philadelphia: University of Pennsylvania Press, 1997), pp. 208–317, esp. 268.

61. The historical narrative here owes a great debt to the following works: Chris Given-Wilson, *The Royal Household*; Anthony Goodman, *John of Gaunt: The Exercise of Power in Fourteenth-Century Europe* (New York: St. Martin's Press, 1992); Nigel Saul, *Richard II*

(New Haven, CT: Yale University Press, 1997); and Simon Walker, *The Lancastrian Affinity*.

62. B. Prol. 149–51.

63. Kennedy "Retaining," p. 209. For further discussion about the violent implications of "game" and "play" here, see "Retaining," note 35.

64. B. Prol. 160–62.

65. B. Prol. 162–63. I discuss the significance of alluding to retainers as dogs on p. 76.

66. B. Prol. 190.

67. See Doris Fletcher, "The Lancastrian Collar of Esses: Its Origins and Transformations Down the Ages," in *The Age of Richard II*, ed. James Gillespie (New York: St. Martin's Press, 1997), pp. 191–204, for details about Gaunt's livery collar.

68. Goodman, *John of Gaunt*, p. 312.

69. Walker, *Lancastrian*, p. 204. In fact, Derby used both the Lancastrian SS collar, as well as other tokens. Walker, *Lancastrian*, p. 94.

70. Chris Given-Wilson, ed. *The Chronicle of Adam Usk 1377–1421* (Oxford: Clarendon Press, 1997), p. 53. More common tokens of Derby's lordship were the antelope, white swan, and fox's brush, but Thompson insists that "here, however, is the badge of the greyhound, so specifically named that there can be no doubt that Henry made use of it": Edward Maunde Thompson, ed. *Chronicon Adae de Usk A.D. 1377–1421* (London: Henry Frowde, 1904), p. 173 n.2.

71. R.L. Storey, "Liveries and Commissions of the Peace 1388–90," in *The Reign of Richard II. Essays in Honour of May McKisack*, ed. F.R.H. Du Boulay and Caroline M. Barron (London: University of London, 1971), pp. 131–52.

72. Walker, *Lancastrian*, p. 13. C. Prol. 176, 179.

73. C. Prol. 211.

74. For discussion of the Lancastrian affinity under Henry IV, see especially Bean, *From Lord to Patron*; Biggs, "Henry IV and His JP's"; Brown, "Henry IV"; Given-Wilson, "Royal Household."

75. For a cogent overview of late-fourteenth- and fifteenth-century legislation concerning livery and maintenance, see J.M.W. Bean, *From Lord to Patron*, generally, but be aware that Bean is working from a very narrow set of definitions.

76. Text from Helen Barr, ed. *The Piers Plowman Tradition A Critical Edition of* Pierce the Ploughman's Crede, Richard the Redeless, Mum and the Sothsegger, *and* The Crowned King (London: J.M. Dent, 1993). See Barr's notes to these lines for her identifications of individual

lines with individual articles. Citations to *Richard the Redeless* will be to passus and line number.

77. RR. 1. 96–106. For the Record and Process, see Rot. Parl. iii 416–22, or see Chris Given-Wilson, trans. *Chronicles of the Revolution, 1397–1400: The Reign of Richard II* (Manchester: Manchester University Press, 1993).

78. Of course, the *Richard*-poet may simply be borrowing from anti-Ricardian tradition, or a common understanding of Richard's regime's faults for this list. Nevertheless, its similarity to the Articles of Deposition is suggestive, considering the efforts Henry made to publish these Articles. Barr sees similarities also. See Helen Barr, *Signes and Sothe: Language in the* Piers Plowman *Tradition* (Cambridge: D.S. Brewer, 1994), especially pp. 159–60. Diane Facinelli notes similarities in *Mum and the Sothsegger* but not in *Richard*; see "Treasonous Criticism of Henry IV: The Loyal Poet of *Richard the Redeless* and *Mum and the Sothsegger*," *Journal of the Rocky Mountain Medieval and Renaissance Association* 10 (1989): 51–65.

79. Rot. Parl. iii 420b.

80. Here I differ with James Dean, when he interprets this to mean "by appraising of pole-axis": James M. Dean, ed. *Richard the Redeless and Mum and the Sothsegger* (Kalamazoo, MI: Medieval Institute Publications, 2000), p. 26.

81. I find both the OED and the MED support reading "owing" for "dette" and "dias" for "dees" more closely than "debt" and "dice" that Dean suggests (p. 26).

82. RR. 1. 85. The *Richard*-poet returns to the Articles of Deposition at the beginning of passus 4. Here he discusses the inability of Richard to pay the debts of his household out of royal income (IV. 1–13, Articles 18 and 32), taxation in peacetime (IV. 14–19, Article 32), and disruption of traditional selection of sheriffs and shire knights (IV. 28–29, Articles 30, 36 and 37).

83. RR. 2. 1–2.

84. RR. 2. 21, 29, 38.

85. RR. 2. 47. This line of argument may have held some currency at the time, as it appears in a parliamentary petition of about 1400, and the ethics of a retinue at once royal and private was questioned generally. See John Watts, "Looking for the State in Medieval England," in *Heraldry, Pageantry and Social Display in Medieval England*, ed. Peter Coss and Maurice Keen (Woodbridge, Suffolk: Boydell Press, 2002), pp. 243–67, esp. 266.

86. RR. 2. 50–51.

87. RR. 2. 57.
88. RR. 2. 40.
89. RR. 2. 135–38.
90. RR. 2. 77–90. Barr considers this to be a passage about the judiciary, and while nobles did act as JPs, I think this passage is more correctly read as one about the nobility. Barr, "Sothe," p. 137.
91. To livery menial servants remained legal, but generally these men benefited from a different level of public power than mid- and upper-level retainers.
92. RR. 2. 83–84, 86.
93. RR. 2. 89.
94. RR. 2. 140–42. This image also calls to mind that of the Virgin of Misericord images where her people are protected under her cloak.
95. RR. 2. 3–7.
96. Bean, *From Lord to Patron*, p. 210.
97. Recall that textual citations are from Bergen, *Fall of Princes*, citing book and line numbers. Citations to notes cite volume and page.
98. *Fall*, VIII, 2420–64, also see note to these lines.
99. Richard A. Dwyer, "Arthur's Stellification in the *Fall of Princes*," *Philological Quarterly* 57 (1978): 155–71.
100. Bergen IV, p. 326. Bergen includes the French version of the Arthuriad in the notes.
101. For a scholarly discussion of the political uses for the chivalric orders, see Hugh Collins, "The Order of the Garter, 1348–1461: Chivalry and Politics in Later Medieval England," in *Courts, Counties, and the Capital in the Later Middle Ages*, ed. Diana Dunn (New York: St. Martin's Press, 1996), pp. 155–80.
102. The French has "certaines loix et ordonnances," but Lydgate greatly expands on the nature of the duties and on the bureaucratic reality of them. Bergen IV, p. 331.
103. In the French, the knights swear to remove their armor only at night while sleeping, to seek out "aduentures merueileuses," to defend with all their strength the weak, and to never refuse help to any who asked it, to do no violence, nor to do any offense or harm to any of their fellow knights of the Round Table, to work towards the well-being of their fellow knights, to risk their lives for their country, to seek out honor, to never break their faith for any reason whatsoever, to honor religion diligently, and to give welcome to poor, honest travelers. Bergen IV, p. 331.

104. *Fall*, VIII, 2741–42.

105. *Fall*, VIII, 2745–50.

106. One has to wonder if this is not praise for those who assisted Henry IV against Richard II years earlier.

107. *Fall*, VIII, 2751–57.

108. *Fall*, VIII, 2761–70.

109. *Fall*, VIII, 2759. For Laurent's version of this passage, see the note in Bergen IV, p. 331.

110. For critics with this understanding, see for example Helen Cooper, ed. *Le Morte Darthur The Winchester Manuscript* (Oxford: Oxford University Press, 1998); Raluca Radulescu credits Richard Barber's article "Malory's *Le Morte Darthur* and Court Culture," *Arthurian Literature* 12 (1993): 133–55 with being the definitive article on the topic in *The Gentry Context*, p. 85n7. It should be noted that the Malorian oath resembles a list of injunctions given to the new Bath knights, not an oath per se.

111. *Fall*, VIII, 2736, 2738, 2780–81.

112. For a recent lengthy study of the medieval Order of the Garter, see Hugh E.L. Collins, *The Order of the Garter 1348–1461* (Oxford: Clarendon Press, 2000). Collins notes that Lydgate was familiar enough with the Order to have included discussion of it in his poem "The Legend of St. George" in the later 1420s (p. 262).

113. Scholarly treatments of the Knights of the Bath are unfortunately few, and most recent scholars defer to Anstis: John Anstis, *Observations Introductory to an Historical Essay, Upon the Knighthood of the Bath* (London: James Woodman, 1725). One of the rare studies that makes use of Anstis, and also includes much original research, is Fionn Pilbrow, "The Knights of the Bath: Dubbing to Knighthood in Lancastrian and Yorkist England," in *Heraldry, Pageantry and Social Display in Medieval England*, ed. Peter Coss and Maurice Keen (Woodbridge, Suffolk: Boydell Press, 2002), pp. 195–218.

114. Appendix C in Harold Arthur, Viscount Dillon, "A Manuscript Collection of Ordinances of Chivalry of the Fifteenth Century," *Archaeologia* 57 (1900): 29–70.

115. *Fall*, VIII, 2752–54.

116. For a sample of work on the perils of wardship, see Noël James Menuge, "Female Wards and Marriage in Romance and Law: A Question of Consent," in *Young Medieval Women*, ed. Katherine J. Lewis, Noël James Menuge, and Kim Phillips (New York: St. Martin's Press, 1999), pp. 153–71; Saunders, *Rape and*

Ravishment, gives some interesting examples on pp. 68–70; Sue Sheridan Walker, "Punishing Convicted Ravishers: Statutory Strictures and Actual Practice in Thirteenth and Fourteenth-Century England," *Journal of Medieval History* 13 (1987): 237–50.

117. *Fall*, VIII, 2822.

118. *Fall*, VIII, 2743–44.

119. This is implicit in

> Also ye schall sitte ī noo plase where that eny iugement schulde be gevyn wrongefully ayens eny body to yowre knowleche....
>
> with yowre power ye schall lete doo take [criminals] and put them in to the handis of Justice and that they be punysshid as the kyngis lawe woll.

quoted earlier, as it emphasizes that the Knights of the Bath are to recognize and redress any legal situations corrupted by influence, and not take the law into their own hands, but use their power to make sure indicted criminals make it to royal courts for sentencing.

120. *Fall*, VIII, 2779, emphasis mine.

121. Richard Firth Green, "Palamon's Appeal of Treason in the *Knight's Tale*," in *The Letter of the Law: Legal Practice and Literary Production in Medieval England*, ed. Emily Steiner and Candace Barrington (Ithaca, NY: Cornell University Press, 2002), pp. 105–14.

122. *Fall*, VIII, 2848–49.

123. 1 Stat. 8 RII c. 5.

124. For additional information, see G.D. Squibb, *The High Court of Chivalry* (Oxford: Clarendon Press, 1959).

125. For an insightful exploration of the deepening understanding of politics in the fifteenth century, including Lydgate's deployment of "pollecie" in the Lancastrian cause, see Paul Strohm, *Politique: Languages of Statecraft between Chaucer and Shakespeare* (Notre Dame, IN: University of Notre Dame Press, 2005).

126. *Fall*, VIII, 2805–6, 2827–28.

127. *Fall*, VIII, 2807.

128. See Strohm, *Politique*, for a discussion of the contemporary understanding of the necessity of "dowblenesse" at a time of protracted civil unrest.

129. Bean, *Lord to Patron*, p. 217. For a slightly different perspective, see Michael Hicks, "The 1468 Statute of Livery," *Historical Research* 64 (1991): 15–28.

5 Maintaining Justice

1. Recent scholarly consensus agrees that Gower was probably a lawyer or other legal official. See for example, John Hines, Nathalie Cohen, and Simon Roffey, "Iohannes Gower, Armiger, Poeta: Life Records and Memorials of His Life and Death," in *A Companion to Gower*, ed. Siân Echard (Cambridge: D.S. Brewer, 2004), pp. 23–43. Compare this with older impressions in Eric Stockton, trans. *The Major Latin Works of John Gower* (Seattle: University of Washington, Seattle, 1962), p. 220n1, or John Fisher, *John Gower Moral Philosopher and Friend of Chaucer* (New York: New York University Press, 1964), p. 107.

2. For information about the legal profession, see especially J.H. Baker, ed. *The Order of Serjeants of Law* (London: Seldon Society, 1984); John Bellamy, *Crime and Public*, and *Bastard Feudalism*; Paul Brand, *Origins of the Legal Profession* (Oxford: Blackwell, 1992); Anthony Musson, *Medieval Law in Context*; Robert C. Palmer, *The County Courts of Medieval England, 1150–1350* (Princeton: Princeton University Press, 1982), and *English Law in the Age of the Black Death, 1348–1381* (Chapel Hill, NC: University of North Carolina Press, 1993). For a view denying that a fourteenth-century legal profession existed, see N.L. Ramsey, "What Was the Legal Profession?" in *Profit, Piety, and the Professions in Later Medieval England*, ed. Michael Hicks (Gloucester: Alan Sutton, 1990), pp. 62–71.

3. I am grateful to Richard Firth Green for pointing me to the *Speculum Vitae*. For this discussion of the *Speculum Vitae* I used British Museum Additional 33995 (the Simeon ms), checked against BM Add. 22283 (the Vernon ms), Bodleian Eng. Poet 5, and Bod. Lyell 28. Lacking a modern edition of the *Speculum Vitae*, citations are to folios in BM Add. 33995. For further examples of shorter, earlier poems including criticism of the legal profession, see for example "London Lickpenney," and "The Simonie," in James M. Dean, ed. *Medieval English Political Writings* (Kalamazoo, MI: Western Michigan University, 1996), pp. 222–25, and 193–212.

4. BM. Add. 33995. f. 41b. Sounding as similar as it does to Chaucer's Miller's caution that "ther be ful goode wyves many oon,/ And evere a thousand goode ayens oon badde" (MT 3154–55), it is easy to be skeptical of this caveat, however.

5. Nassington includes officials found in both common and ecclesiastical courts, but in keeping with the rest of this book, I will restrict my comments to common law officials.

6. BM. Add. 33995. f. 41a. I am expanding abbreviations silently.

7. BM. Add. 33995. f. 41a.

8. BM. Add. 33995. f. 41a.

9. BM. Add. 33995. f. 41a.

10. BM. Add. 33995. f. 41b.

11. BM. Add. 33995. f. 41b.

12. BM. Add. 33995. f. 41b.

13. BM. Add. 33995. f. 41b.

14. BM. Add. 33995. f. 41b. Nassington discusses "fals sissours" in two places, once near witnesses, and once near judges. I suspect this reflects the varied nature of jurors' duties; they served on indicting juries (in the first instance), but also on trial juries (in the second instance).

15. See, for example, the extended discussions in Maddicott, *Law and Lordship*, Biggs, "Plantagenet," and Musson, *Context*.

16. Maddicott, *Law and Lordship*, pp. 55–56. Musson, *Context*, pp. 63–64 says something very similar.

17. Maddicott, *Law and Lordship*, p. 80.

18. Indeed, the letters provide further evidence for Biggs' contention that bureaucrats, lawyers, and judges continued to benefit from retaining under Henry IV and Henry V.

19. Edward Powell, *Kingship, Law, and Society: Criminal Justice in the Reign of Henry V* (Oxford: Clarendon Press, 1989), p. 274.

20. *Mirour* 24493–95. Wilson, *Gower*, p. 321. Macaulay, *Complete Works*. In the following discussion, I will quote from the French and provide Wilson's translations in brackets, and will cite both Macaulay's edition of the French by title and line number, and note Wilson's English translation by page number. William Burton Wilson, trans., *John Gower: Mirour de l'Omme (The Mirror of Mankind)* (East Lansing: Colleagues Press, 1992). The section on lawyers under discussion takes up lines 24181–24624 in Macaulay's text of the *Mirour*, and pages 316–30 in Wilson's translation; chapters 1–5 of Book 6 of the *Vox* deal with lawyers.

   The *Mirour*'s modern translator, William Wilson, attributes Gower's willingness to tamper with gender, declensions, and tenses to meet the demands of his rhyme scheme, but given Gower's familiarity with the law, I wonder if these seeming irregularities may not as well be attributable to a facility in law French, a technical jargon characterized by traits similar to those demonstrated in the *Mirour*. Wilson, Mirour, pp. xxii–xxiii; J.H. Baker, *Manual of Law French Second Edition* (Aldershot: Scolar Press, 1990), pp. 10–15. In 1362, English received a promotion into the courts at the expense of law French, after which date pleading, argument, and judgment were supposed to be in English: pleas were to be recorded in Latin, however (1 Stat. 36 EdwIII c.15). Baker points out that the statute was swiftly ignored, *Manual*, p. 2. For a laudatory discussion of Gower's French works (although he does not discuss the French in the *Mirour* from a philological perspective) see Robert Yeager, "John Gower's French," in *A Companion to Gower*, ed. Sîan Echard (Woodbridge, Suffolk: Boydell, 2004), pp. 137–52.

21. *Mirour* 24241.

22. *Mirour* 24250–52. Wilson, *Gower*, p. 317. See also similar throughout this section.

23. *Mirour* 24260–62, emphasis mine, Wilson, *Gower*, p. 317. Notice that by referring to pleading, Gower is again indicting pleaders in particular.

24. Anne Middleton examines closely the labor legislation involving "confederacies" in "Vagrancy."

25. *Mirour* 24512–14. Wilson, *Gower*, p. 321.

26. The section on judges runs from line 24625–24816 in Macaulay, and pages 323–25 in Wilson, and makes up Book 6, Chapter 5 in the *Vox*.

27. *Vox* 6. 7. Stockton, *Latin*, p. 220. A more literal translation brings out the productive nature of gifts in legal practice: "this work and that effort are brought together primarily through gifts." As with the *Mirour*, I will provide in quotations both the Latin and Stockton's translation.

28. Given-Wilson, PROME. See especially discussion in the parliaments of 1376, 1377, 1378, 1379, January 1380, which resulted in an ordinance concerning the JPs, 1381, October 1382, October 1383, and so on.

29. The section on sheriffs, bailiffs, and jurors runs from line 24817–25176 in Macaulay, and pages 325–30 in Wilson, and makes up Chapter 6 in the *Vox*.

30. *Mirour* 25012–14. Wilson, *Gower*, p. 328. Passages like this one also suggest that Gower is speaking of royal courts rather than county or hundredal jurisdictions, which featured other officials, unmentioned in Gower.

31. Wilson cites Troendle for his own assertion that *traicier* means "one who draws," and connotes "one who packs a jury" in note 129. Troendle does not support her definition, and the absence of a judicial connotation of *traicier* from both the *Anglo-Norman Dictionary* and Baker's glossary of law French casts doubt on Troendle's claim. Dorothy F. Troendle, "Mirour de l'Omme," Dissertation. (Brown

University, 1960), p. 1357. This use of *traicier* may refer to one of the wheel horses in a team, making the analogy one of the entire jury pulling together like a team of horses. Moreover, the wheel horses must pull together: if one leads, the team or pair is pulled out of unison, and it becomes difficult to move the plow or wagon. In using the term, Gower may be reinforcing his point about a *traicier* defeating the smooth motion of justice. Thanks to Carl P. Kennedy for sharing his plowteam driving expertise.

32. *Mirour* 24193–97. Wilson, *Gower*, p. 316.

33. The MED, "laue" definitions 7 a, b shows that one could "bring to law," "put in law," as well as "have law." Moreover, Gower himself discusses the law as a thing at times. See, for example, when he likens the practice of the law to a fowler's snare, a fisherman's hook, and a spider's web (*Vox* 6. 69–72, Stockton 221, *Mirour* 2505–14). Driving the point home, he adds: "causidicus cupidus pavidos de lege propinquos/ Voluit et illaqueat condicioune pari," and then alludes to the "net of the law" (*legis rethe*) (*Vox* 6. 83–84, 86).

34. *Piers Plowman*, C.3.167. "Vult sibi causidicus servare modum meretricis," and "est ita vulgaris domibus via causidicorum" (*Vox* 6. 43, 51). "A common thoroughfare [leads] to lawyers' dwellings" (Stockton 221).

35. *Vox* 6. 68. Stockton, *Latin*, p. 221.

36. *Vox* 6. 175–78. Stockton, *Latin*, p. 224. Also note that this is further evidence for the law being treated as a commodity.

37. Serious attempts were made after the Black Death to restrain social change through regulation of goods and services at the national level, many in an attempt to curb unjust profit. The Ordinance of Laborers (23 EdwIII) and first and second Statutes of Laborers (25 EdwIII, 34 EdwIII) fixed wages, determined terms of service, and stipulated places for hiring. These efforts to legislate labor were built on traditional commercial laws legislating weights and measures like the Assize of Bread and Beer (possibly 51 HenIII) and the Assize of Weights and Measures (possibly 31 EdwI). Concern over value appears again during Edward III's reign, when Parliament passed nearly a dozen statutes or ordinances concerning prices, weights, and measures: 2 EdwIII; 1 Stat. 4 EdwIII c. 3, c. 12; 1 Stat. 14 EdwIII c. 12; 1 Stat. 23 EdwIII; 2 Stat. 25 EdwIII; 5 Stat. 25 EdwIII c. 9–10; 1 Stat. 34 EdwIII c. 5, c. 9–11; 1 Stat. 37 EdwIII c. 3, 1 Stat. 47 EdwIII c. 1.

38. Brand, *Origins*, p. 121.

39. 1 Stat. 3 EdwI c. 29.

40. Baker, *Serjeants*, pp. 46–47.

41. For examples, *Mirour* 24197–24202, 24217–20, 24283–86, 24481–86.

42. *Mirour* 24625–27, and in nearly every passage after that.

43. Baker, *Serjeants*, p. 26.

44. *Piers Plowman*, C. 3. 290–92, 300–304 regarding the distinction between *mede* and *mercede*. Stockton 224–25, *Vox* 185–86, 263–64. Palmer notes that at the county level, at least, pleaders were often granted annuities in the form of cash or land, which was certainly a sort of maintenance. Palmer, *County Courts*, pp. 95, 100. Also see Maddicott, *Law and Lordship*, generally.

45. *Mirour* 24202–04. Wilson, *Gower*, p. 317. I would like to amend this translation to more closely reflect the legal vocabulary of the text that I discuss above: "but they make conspiracies with the rich, and by maintaining cases, they put a price on justice and law."

46. 33 EdwI, Ordinance of Conspirators. The other elements of conspiracy included a pact of mutual aid or falsely maintaining pleas.

47. Nevertheless, recall Brand's cautions. See p. 98.

48. Fisher noted that Gower examines three main themes in each of his major works: individual virtue, legal justice, and the administrative responsibilities of the king, p. 136. Fisher emphasizes the importance of Book 6 of the *Vox Clamantis*, saying that this book is the synthesis of Gower's ideas of law, common profit, and kingship (p. 180).

49. Elizabeth Porter, "Gower's Ethical Microcosm and Political Macrocosm," in *Gower's* Confessio Amantis: *Responses and Reassessments*, ed. A.J. Minnis (Cambridge: D.S. Brewer, 1983), pp. 135–62, esp. 157.

50. Ferster, *Fictions*, p. 134.

51. *Vox* 6. 547–50. Stockton, *Latin*, p. 232.

52. *Vox* 6. 481. Stockton, *Latin*, p. 230.

53. *Vox* 6. 585–86. Stockton, *Latin* p. 233.

54. *Vox* 6. 1067, 1070. "O king, perform your duties to your law," Stockton, *Latin*, p. 245. Literally, the first quote reads as "pay your debts to the law!" We should recall that a *debitum* was also the legal penalty an offender was required to pay, and so I use this more specific translation here.

55. *Vox* 6. 697–700. This translation is my own. Stockton's translation is looser: "the sword is understood as indicating the badge of justice; even so, a king does not lay hold of his weapons in order that a traitor may perish: a king should order such men hauled up high by a noose, lest both his own position and that of the law be destroyed," Stockton, *Latin*, p. 236. My thanks to Richard Firth Green and Frank Coulson for suggestions regarding this passage.

56. For the Ricardian struggle over badges, see Nigel Saul, "The Commons and the Abolition of Badges," *Parliamentary History* 9 (1990): 302–15. For more discussion concerning badges and maintenance, see chapter 4, this book.

57. Middleton, "Vagrancy," p. 226.

58. *Vox* 6. 1169–70. Stockton, *Latin*, p. 248.

59. *Vox* 6. 1177–78. Stockton, *Latin*, p. 248.

60. *Vox* 6. 1187–88, emphasis mine. Stockton, *Latin*, p. 249.

61. *Vox* 6. 1195–96. Stockton, *Latin*, p. 249.

62. R.L. Storey, "Liveries," p. 151. Moreover, by the 1390s it must have begun to be obvious that most of the bench, and a large proportion of the serjeants, were in the pay of Lancaster. See Biggs, "Lancastrianization of Justice," generally.

63. Saul, *Richard*, p. 237.

64. Saul, *Richard*, p. 239.

65. Saul, *Richard*, p. 249.

66. *Vox* 6. 786, Stockton, *Latin*, p. 238.

67. In pursuing this line of argument, I distinguish my research from Ethan Knapp's nuanced analysis of ways in which Hoccleve's bureaucratic background shaped his approach to writing. Fundamentally, the questions that Knapp asks of Hoccleve's texts reveal information about the bureaucrat's psyche, and how he inscribes himself in his texts. In contrast, I am investigating a single work, the *Regiment of Princes*, to determine what the author thought about an institution, the legal profession, of which he was part. See Ethan Knapp, *The Bureaucratic Muse. Thomas Hoccleve and the Literature of Late Medieval England* (University Park, PA: Pennsylvania State University Press, 2001) esp. Chapter 1, "Bureaucratic Identity and the Construction of Self in Hoccleve's *Formulary* and 'La Mal Regle.'" Later, in Chapter 3, "'Wrytynge no travaille is' Scribal Labor in the *Regement of Princes*," Knapp demonstrates that a project like mine is possible, but examines only short portions of the Dialogue with the Old Man; I will begin there, but then continue exploring the rest of the *Regiment*.

68. In general, I think Hoccleve stops short of Toulmie's "poetics of extortion," although the line becomes grey, and reminds us of the mob-analogy used in chapter 1. See Sarah Toulmie, "The *Prive Science* of Thomas Hoccleve," *Studies in the Age of Chaucer* 22 (2000): 281–309.

69. See A.L. Brown, "The Privy Seal Clerks in the Early Fifteenth Century," in *The Study of Medieval Records. Essays in Honour of Kathleen Major*, ed. D.A. Bullough and R.L. Storey (Oxford, Clarendon Press, 1971), pp. 260–81.

70. See Brown, "Clerks," p. 267.

71. I am using Perkins' names for the three divisions of Hoccleve's text (Dialogue with the Old Man, Prologue, and *Regiment*) as they more nearly represent textual divisions as seen in manuscript witnesses than the more traditional Prologue and *Regiment* division: see p. 185 in Nicholas Perkins, *Hoccleve's* Regiment of Princes: *Counsel and Constraint* (Cambridge: D.S. Brewer, 2001) for his defense of this terminology. Citations to the *Regiment* are to line numbers in the TEAMS edition. Charles R. Blyth, ed. *Thomas Hoccleve The Regiment of Princes* (Kalamazoo, MI: Medieval Institute Publications, 1999).

72. Many critics consider confessional angles. For example, Pearsall, who, although he focuses his article elsewhere, considers the Old Man "a kind of confessor" (p. 409), in Derek Pearsall, "Hoccleve's *Regement of Princes:* The Poetics of Royal Self-Representation," *Speculum* 69 (1994): 386–410. Simpson notes confessional overtones, and so does Hasler in James Simpson, "Nobody's Man: Thomas Hoccleve's *Regiment of Princes,*" in *London and Europe in the Later Middle Ages*, ed. Julia Boffey and Pamela King (London: University of London, 1995), pp. 149–80 and Anthony Hasler, "Hoccleve's Unregimented Body," *Paragraph* 13 (1990): 164–81. Like Simpson, Toulmie also sees both Boethian and confessional elements at work here. Even Scanlon gives a nod to a confessional reading of the scene in Larry Scanlon, *Narrative, Authority, and Power. The Medieval Exemplum and the Chaucerian Tradition* (Cambridge: Cambridge University Press, 1994).

73. Knapp, Perkins, and Toulmie, all emphasize economic readings.

74. Perkins, *Counsel and Constraint*, p. 39.

75. Perkins, *Counsel and Constraint*, p. 42.

76. *Regiment* 1487, see Simpson's discussion of this throughout his article. *Regiment* will hereafter be cited as REG.

77. Thus, I must disagree with Simpson: Hoccleve is not trying to become "Henry's man" in the process of writing the *Regiment*, since this form of household maintenance of bureaucrats was far outdated by this time (p. 176).

78. Hasler, "Unregimented," p. 168, Knapp, *Bureaucratic Muse*, p. 89, and Scanlon, *Narrative*, p. 303.

79. REG, 463, 496–97. This criticism is not unique to Hoccleve. In the fifteenth-century romance *Sir Amadace*, Amadace becomes too poor to support his noble lifestyle, and eventually he must even release even his steward, sumpter, and groom from service. See the introduction to the TEAMS edition of *Sir Amadace*. Edward E. Foster,

ed. *Amis and Amiloun, Robert of Cisyle, and Sir Amadace* (Kalamazoo, MI: Western Michigan University Press, 1997).

80. REG, 568–742.

81. Brown "Clerks," p. 262.

82. REG, 793–94.

83. REG, 801–3, 821–22, 825.

84. See Toulmie, *"Prive Scilence,"* pp. 287–88, 291 and Perkins, *Counsel and Constraint*, p. 149 for related discussions.

85. REG, 988–89, 993.

86. REG, 997–1015.

87. REG, 1019–22.

88. For a traditional discussion of the indentured army, see Richard Ager Newhall, *Muster and Review: A Problem of English Military Administration 1420–1440* (Cambridge: Harvard University Press, 1940).

89. REG, 841.

90. J.L. Kirby, *Henry IV of England* (London: Archon Books, 1971). Kirby notes that the issue of Henry's unpaid annuities was so pressing that until the 1407 parliament it had been his policy to pay the oldest first, but then in 1407 he determined to pay those held by his day-to-day employees first, and the rest if there were funds remaining (p. 217).

91. REG, 1500.

92. REG, 1501–3.

93. REG, 1509–12.

94. REG, 1515, 1517–18.

95. See Perkins' Section 3 for a breakdown of the sources of Hoccleve's stories.

96. See Kathleen E. Kennedy, "Hoccleve's Dangerous Game of Draughts," *Notes and Queries* N.S., 53 (2006): 410–14, esp. 411.

97. Kennedy, "Draughts," p. 411.

98. In the late fifteenth century this story provided the material for two large panel-paintings by Gerard David for the council room of Bruges. It is notable that in David's version, the judge explicitly takes a bribe.

99. Scanlon, *Narrative*, p. 286.

100. Perkins, *Counsel and Constraint*, p. 140.

101. In Gower's version, the judge is simply "laweles" and Cambyses accuses him of "coveitise," leaving the judge's acceptance of bribery or maintenance implied, rather than stated (CA, 2894, 2903). In both Gower's and Hoccleve's version of the Judgment of Cambyses the judge acts upon his own discretion, instead of

following the law, and is punished for it in a manner meant as a caution to other judges, especially his successor to the position. The king matches the judge's arbitrariness by ordering the judge flayed; no trial is mentioned. As Gower pointedly remarks: "in defalte of other jugge/ The king mot otherwhile jugge,/ To holden up the rihte lawe" (CA, VII, 2905–7). For this tale in *Confessio Amantis*, see Book 7, lines 2889–2907.

102. REG, 2677. Nevertheless, de Cessolis also fails to mention a bribe in the story, and focuses instead on "rightwisnesse," as does Hoccleve in line 2688. As I mention above, however, Gower does imply that the judge's corruption is financially based. Apparatus in extant manuscripts suggests also that this *exemplum* was understood to be about judicial payment, and this story includes more Latin marginal glosses than most other sections of the *Regiment*, suggesting this theme was of importance to Hoccleve. The glosses are drawn either from the Bible or various collections of decretals.

103. REG, 2689–90.

104. REG, 2696–98.

105. REG, 2703–6.

106. If the bench had been in the pay of Lancaster for decades, this may explain why public complaint lessened in the 1390s, then grew again in the early fifteenth century. As I discuss at length in chapter 4 above, the House of Lancaster went from the richest noble house in the fourteenth century to enrich itself with the royal holdings as well in 1399. Poor financial administration, however, left the now royal house unable to pay the annuities owed its retainers soon after 1399. The same lack of adequate remuneration that drove the judiciary to accept fees in the 1370s and 1380s may have driven them to accept fees again in the early fifteenth century.

107. REG, 3112–13.

108. REG, 3116–17.

109. REG, 3121–22.

110. Richard, of course, had been infamous for selling pardons. Nevertheless, the number of pardons for felonies rose after 1399, probably because they were lucrative for Henry IV's cash-strapped regime; in fact, Henry encouraged pardon-seekers by issuing a number of general pardons. The number of pardons issued fell in the reigns of Henry V and VI. See Bellamy, *Criminal Trial*.

111. REG, 3135–36.

112. REG, 3149.
113. REG, 3151–52.
114. REG, 3161.
115. Kennedy, "Draughts," p. 412.
116. Bellamy, *Criminal Trial*, p. 139. See also T.F. Tout, *Chapters in the Administrative History of Mediæval England* (Manchester: Manchester University Press, 1930) volume 5, pp. 57–58, for a more extended explanation of the Privy Seal's role in issuing warrants.
117. REG, 3182.
118. REG, 3191–92.
119. REG, 3270.
120. REG, 3272–77.
121. REG, 3276.
122. REG, 3284. In Middle English, *advocat* could mean either an attorney or a pleader (barrister); however, given the context here, when Caesar literally puts his body in court for his knight's: "advocat wole I be in my persone/ For thee," I suggest that attorney is the intended meaning (pp. 3295–96).
123. REG, 3297.
124. True, few juries would be likely to convict anyone represented by the emperor, but legal forms are being kept more strictly here. It should be noted that as an attorney Caesar would have a more minimal presence in court than would the pleader for the knight's case.
125. See Toulmie, *"Prive Scilence,"* pp. 287–88, 291, for a discussion of Hoccleve as a "bureaucratic warrior" and the parallels Hoccleve makes between soldiering and clerking as well as how bureaucratic work embodied the royal will. Also consider Perkins' discussion of the parallel between the knight's showing of his wounds and Hoccleve's body on p. 149.
126. REG, 3299–3300. It is also worth noting that an analogue of this tale exists in Gower's *Confessio Amantis*, Book 7, lines 2061–2114. In this, the knight is suing to recover his right, and is in no danger of execution. Caesar appoints him legal counsel, but does not appear to take his turn as an attorney. Instead he "tok his cause on honde" and gave the knight a living of some sort: "he yaf him good ynough to spende/ For evere unto his lives ende" (CA, VII, 2103, 2105–6). Unlike Hoccleve, here Gower seems to advocate traditional means of remuneration.
127. Paul Strohm, *England's Empty Throne. Usurpation and the Language of Legitimation, 1399–1422* (London: Yale University Press, 1998), p. 213.

128. Perkins, *Counsel and Constraint*, p. 113.

129. Scanlon, *Narrative*, p. 319.

130. Scanlon, *Narrative*, p. 321.

131. Perkins, *Counsel and Constraint*, pp. 112–13. Scanlon, *Narrative*, p. 320.

132. Scanlon notes that Hoccleve's audience would have consisted of "the nobility and urban patrichiate—the audience of the Chaucerian tradition," but manuscript evidence alone suggests a wider readership, including bureaucrats, see Scanlon, *Narrative*, p. 319, and Perkins, *Counsel and Constraint*, p. 174. Furthermore, each side could construct a reading preferential to their own group; as Simpson says, "power predetermines interpretation," Simpson, "Man," p. 155.

133. REG, 4348–54.

134. REG, 4204.

135. REG, 4340.

136. Strohm, *Empty Throne*, p. 210.

137. Scanlon, *Narrative*, pp. 320–21.

138. REG, 4366–67.

139. REG, 4383–86.

140. MED, "guerdoun," "annuitee."

141. REG, 4353–54.

142. REG, 4404–6, 4411–17.

BIBLIOGRAPHY

Primary Works

Manuscripts

British Museum Additional 22283.
British Museum Additional 33995.
Oxford Bodleian Eng. Poet 5.
Oxford Bodleian Lyell 28.

Printed

Baildon, William, ed. *Select Cases in Chancery A.D.1364–1471.* Seldon Society 10. London: Seldon Society, 1896.

Barr, Helen, ed. *The Piers Plowman Tradition A Critical Edition of* Pierce the Ploughman's Crede, Richard the Redeless, Mum and the Sothsegger, *and* The Crowned King. London: J.M. Dent, 1993.

Benson, Larry, ed. *The Riverside Chaucer.* 3rd ed. Boston: Houghton Mifflin, 1987.

Bergen, Henry. *Lydgate's Fall of Princes.* 4 vols. Oxford: Oxford University Press, 1967.

———, ed. *Lydgate's Troy Book, A.D. 1412–20.* London: Early English Texts Society, 1906–1935.

Blyth, Charles R. ed. *Thomas Hoccleve The Regiment of Princes.* Kalamazoo, MI: Medieval Institute Publications, 1999.

Carpenter, Christine, ed. *The Armburgh Papers: The Brokholes Inheritance in Warwickshire, Hertfordshire, and Essex c.1417–1453.* Woodbridge, Suffolk: The Boydell Press, 1998.

———, ed. *Kingsford's Stonor Letters and Papers 1290–1483.* Cambridge: Cambridge University Press, 1996.

Cooper, Helen, ed. *Le Morte Darthur The Winchester Manuscript.* Oxford: Oxford University Press, 1998.

Davis, Norman, ed. *Paston Letters and Papers of the Fifteenth Century.* 2 vols. Oxford: Clarendon Press, 1971.

Dean, James M., ed. *Richard the Redeless and Mum and the Sothsegger.* Kalamazoo, MI: Medieval Institute Publications, 2000.

———. *Medieval English Political Writings.* Kalamazoo, MI: Western Michigan University, 1996.

Foster, Edward E., ed. *Amis and Amiloun, Robert of Cisyle, and Sir Amadace.* Kalamazoo, MI: Western Michigan University Press, 1997.

Given-Wilson, Chris., ed. *The Chronicle of Adam Usk 1377–1421.* Oxford: Clarendon Press, 1997.

———, ed. and trans. *Chronicles of the Revolution, 1397–1400: The Reign of Richard II.* Manchester: Manchester University Press, 1993.

———, ed. *The Parliament Rolls of Medieval England.* Leicester, UK: Scholarly Digital Editions, 2005.

Hahn, Thomas, ed. *Sir Gawain: Eleven Romances and Tales.* Kalamazoo, MI: Medieval Institute Publications, 1995.

Harwood, Alfred J., ed. *Year Books of the Reign of King Edward the Third.* London: His Majesty's Stationary Office, 1896.

Hecher, L.C., and Michael Hecher, eds. *Year Books of Richard II. 8–10 Richard II 1385–1387.* London: Ames Foundation, 1987.

Kane, George, ed. *Piers Plowman: The A-Version.* London: University of London Press, 1960.

Macaulay, G.C., ed. *The Complete Works of John Gower.* 4 vols. Oxford: Clarendon Press, 1902.

McSparran, Frances, chief ed. *The Electronic Middle English Dictionary.* Ann Arbor, MI: University of Michigan Press, 2001.

Pearsall, Derek, ed. *Piers Plowman the C-text.* 1978; corrected ed. Exeter: University of Exeter Press, 1999.

Russell, George, and George Kane, eds. *Will's Visions of Piers Plowman, Do-Well, Do-Better, Do-Best.* London: Athalone, 1997.

Schmidt, A.V.C., ed. *The Vision of Piers Plowman.* 1995; new ed. repr. London: J.M. Dent, 1998.

Simpson, John, chief ed. *Oxford English Dictionary.* Oxford: University of Oxford Press, 2007.

Stapleton, Thomas, ed. *The Plumpton Correspondence.* Gloucester: Alan Sutton, 1990.

The Statutes of the Realm (1225–1713) Printed by Command of His Majesty King George the Third. London: G. Eyre and A. Strahan, 1810–2.

Stockton, Eric, ed. and trans. *The Major Latin Works of John Gower.* Seattle: University of Washington, Press, 1962.

Thompson, Edward Maunde, ed. *Chronicon Adae de Usk A.D. 1377–1421.* London: Henry Frowde, 1904.

Thornley, Isobel, ed. *Year Books of II Richard II 1387–1388.* London: Spottiswood, Ballantyne, & Co., 1937.

Wilson, William Burton, trans. *John Gower: Mirour de l'Omme (The Mirror of Mankind)*. East Lansing, MI: Colleagues Press, 1992.

Wulfing, J. Ernst, ed. *The Laud Troy Book*. Millwood, NY: Early English Text Society, Kraus Reprint, 1988.

Secondary Works

Unpublished Secondary Works

Troendle, Dorothy F. "Mirour de l'Omme." Dissertation. Brown University, 1960.

Published Secondary Works

Aers, David, and Lynn Staley. *Powers of the Holy: Religion, Politics, and Gender in Late Medieval English Culture*. University Park, PA: Pennsylvania State Press, 1996.

Alford, John. *Piers Plowman: A Glossary of Legal Diction*. Cambridge: D.S. Brewer, 1988.

Anstis, John. *Observations Introductory to an Historical Essay, Upon the Knighthood of the Bath*. London: James Woodman, 1725.

Archer, Rowena. "'How Ladies…Who Live on Their Manors Ought to Manage Their Households and Estates' Women as Landholders and Administrators in the Later Middle Ages," in *Women in English Society c. 1200–1500*. Ed. P.J.P. Goldberg. Stroud, Gloucestershire: Alan Sutton, 1992. pp. 149–81.

Attreed, Lorraine. "Arbitration and the Growth of Urban Liberties in Late Medieval England." *Journal of British Studies*. 31 (1992) 205–35.

Avery, Margaret. "The History of the Equitable Jurisdiction of Chancery before 1460." *Bulletin of the Institute for Historical Research*. 42 (1969) 129–44.

Baker, J.H. *An Introduction to English Legal History*. 4th edn. London: Butterworths, 2002.

———. *Manual of Law French Second Edition*. Aldershot: Scolar Press, 1990.

———. *The Order of Serjeants of Law*. London: Seldon Society, 1984.

Baldwin, Anna. *The Theme of Government in* Piers Plowman. Cambridge: D.S. Brewer, 1981.

Barber, Richard. "Malory's *Le Morte Darthur* and Court Culture." *Arthurian Literature*. 12 (1993) 133–55.

Barr, Helen. *Signes and Sothe: Language in the* Piers Plowman *Tradition*. Cambridge: D.S. Brewer, 1994.

Baswell, Christopher, and Paul Beekman Taylor. "The *Faire Queene Eleyne* in Chaucer's *Troilus*." *Speculum*. 63 (1988) 293–311.

Bean, J.M.W. *From Lord to Patron: Lordship in Late Medieval England.* Manchester: Manchester University Press, 1989.

Beilby, Mark. "The Profits of Expertise: The Rise of the Civil Lawyers and Chancery Equity," in *Profit, Piety, and the Professions in Later Medieval England.* Ed. Michael Hicks. Gloucester: Alan Sutton, 1990. pp. 72–90.

Bellamy, J.G. *Bastard Feudalism and the Law.* Portland, OR: Aeropagitica Press, 1989.

——. *Crime and Public Order in England in the Later Middle Ages.* London: Routledge, 1973.

——. *The Criminal Trial in Later Medieval England.* Toronto: University of Toronto Press, 1998.

Bennett, J.A.W. "The Date of the B-Text of *Piers Plowman.*" *Medium Ævum.* 12 (1943) 55–64.

Bennett, Josephine W. "The Mediaeval Loveday." *Speculum.* 33 (1958) 351–70.

Benson, C. David. *The History of Troy in Middle English Literature.* Woodbridge, Suffolk: D.S. Brewer, 1980.

Bertholet, Craig. "From Revenge to Reform: The Changing Face of 'Lucrece' and Its Meaning in Gower's *Confessio Amantis.*" *Philological Quarterly.* 70 (1991) 403–21.

Biebel, Elizabeth. "A Wife, a Batterer, and a Rapist: Representations of "Masculinity" in the *Wife of Bath's Prologue* and *Tale,*" in *Masculinities in Chaucer: Approaches to Maleness in the* Canterbury Tales *and* Troilus and Criseyde. Ed. Peter Beidler. Cambridge: Brewer, 1998. pp. 63–75.

Biggs, Douglas. "Henry IV and His JP's: The Lancastrianization of Justice, 1399–1413," in *Traditions and Transformations in Fifteenth Century England.* Ed. Sharon Michalove and Douglas Biggs. Boston: Brill, 2002. pp. 59–79.

——. "A Plantagenet Revolution in Government? The Officers of Central Government and the Lancastrian Usurpation of 1399." *Medieval Prosopography.* 20 (1999): 191–212.

——. *Three Armies in Britain: The Irish Campaign of Richard II and the Usurpation of Henry IV, 1397–99.* Leiden: Brill, 2007.

Blanch, Robert J. " 'Al Was This Land Fulfild of Fayereye': The Thematic Employment of Force, Willfulness, and Legal Conventions in Chaucer's *Wife of Bath's Tale.*" *Studia Neophilologica.* 57 (1985) 41–51.

Bloch, R. Howard. "Chaucer's Maiden's Head: The *Physician's Tale* and the Poetics of Virginity." *Representations.* 28 (1989) 113–34.

Bott, Robin L. " 'O, Keep Me From That Worse Than Killing Lust,' Ideologies of Rape and Mutilation in Chaucer's *Physician's Tale* and

Shakespeare's *Titus Andronicus*," in *Representing Rape in Medieval and Early Modern English Literature*. Ed. Elizabeth Robertson and Christine M. Rose. New York: Palgrave, 2001. pp. 189–211.

Brand, Paul. *The Origins of the Legal Profession*. Oxford: Blackwell, 1992.

Brown, A.L. "The Privy Seal Clerks in the Early Fifteenth Century," in *The Study of Medieval Records. Essays in Honour of Kathleen Major*. Ed. D.A. Bullough and R.L. Storey. Oxford: Clarendon Press, 1971. pp. 260–81.

———. "The Reign of Henry IV," in *Fifteenth-Century England 1399– 1509 Studies in Politics and History*. Ed. S.B. Chrimes, C.D. Ross, and R.A. Griffiths. Manchester, Manchester University Press, 1972. pp. 1–28.

Brown, Carole Koepke. "Episodic Patterns and the Perpetrator: The Structure and Meaning of Chaucer's *Wife of Bath's Tale*." *Chaucer Review*. 31 (1996) 18–35.

Burrow, J.A. "Lady Meed and the Power of Money." *Medium Ævum*. 75 (2005) 113–18.

Burton, T.L. "The Wife of Bath's Fourth and Fifth Husbands and Her Ideal Sixth: The Growth of a Marital Philosophy." *Chaucer Review*. 13 (1979) 34–50.

Burger, Glenn. *Chaucer's Queer Nation*. Minneapolis, MN: University of Minnesota Press, 2003.

Cannon, Christopher. "Chaucer and Rape: Uncertainty's Certainties," in *Representing Rape in Medieval and Early Modern Literature*. Ed. Elizabeth Robertson and Christine Rose. New York: Palgrave, 2001. pp. 255–79.

———. "*Raptus* in the Chaumpaigne Release and a Newly Discovered Document Concerning the Life of Geoffrey Chaucer." *Speculum*. 68 (1993): 74–94.

Carpenter, Christine. *Locality and Polity: A Study of Warwickshire Landed Society, 1401–1499*. Cambridge: Cambridge University Press, 1992.

———. "The Stonor Circle in the Fifteenth Century," in *Rulers and Ruled in Late Medieval England*. Ed. Rowena Archer and Simon Walker. London: Hambledon Press, 1995. pp. 175–200.

Clanchy, Michael. "Law and Love in the Middle Ages," in *Disputes and Settlements*. Ed. John Bossy. Cambridge: Cambridge University Press, 1983. pp. 47–67.

Clayton, Dorothy J. "Peace Bonds and the Maintenance of Law and Order in Late Medieval England: The Example of Cheshire." *Bulletin of the Institute of Historical Research*. 58 (1985) 133–48.

Collins, Hugh. *The Order of the Garter 1348–1461*. Oxford: Clarendon Press, 2000.

Collins, Hugh. "The Order of the Garter, 1348–1461: Chivalry and Politics in Later Medieval England," in *Courts, Counties, and the Capital in the Later Middle Ages*. Ed. Diana Dunn. New York: St. Martin's Press, 1996. pp. 155–80.

Crane, Susan. "The Franklin as Dorigen." *Chaucer Review*. 24 (1990) 236–52.

Viscount Dillon, Harold Arthur. "A Manuscript Collection of Ordinances of Chivalry of the Fifteenth Century." *Archaeologia*. 57 (1900) 29–70.

Dobyns, Ann. "Chaucer and the Rhetoric of Justice." *Disputatio*. 4 (1999) 75–89.

Dwyer, Richard A. "Arthur's Stellification in the *Fall of Princes*." *Philological Quarterly*. 57 (1978) 155–71.

Facinelli, Diane. "Treasonous Criticism of Henry IV: The Loyal Poet of *Richard the Redeless* and *Mum and the Sothsegger*." *Journal of the Rocky Mountain Medieval and Renaissance Association*. 10 (1989) 51–65.

Farber, Lianna. "The Creation of Consent in the *Physician's Tale*." *Chaucer Review*. 39 (2004) 151–64.

Ferster, Judith. *Fictions of Advice. The Literature of Counsel in Late Medieval England*. Philadelphia: University of Pennsylvania Press, 1996.

Fewer, Colin. "John Lydgate's *Troy Book* and the Ideology of Prudence." *Chaucer Review*. 38 (2004) 229–45.

Fisher, John. *John Gower Moral Philosopher and Friend of Chaucer*. New York: New York University Press, 1964.

Fletcher, Doris. "The Lancastrian Collar of Esses: Its Origins and Transformations Down the Ages," in *The Age of Richard II*. Ed. James Gillespie. New York: St. Martin's Press, 1997. pp. 191–204.

Fowler, Elizabeth. "Civil Death and the Maiden: Agency and the Conditions of Contract in *Piers Plowman*." *Speculum*. 70 (1995) 760–92.

Fyler, John M. "Love and Degree in the *Franklin's Tale*." *Chaucer Review*. 21 (1987) 321–37.

Giancarlo, Matthew. *Parliament and Literature in Late Medieval England*. Cambridge: Cambridge University Press, 2007.

Given-Wilson, Chris. *The Royal Household and the King's Affinity: Service, Politics and Finance in England, 1360–1413*. New York: Yale University Press, 1986.

Goodman, Anthony. *John of Gaunt: The Exercise of Power in Fourteenth-Century Europe*. New York: St. Martin's Press, 1992.

Green, Richard Firth. "Chaucer's Victimized Women." *Studies in the Age of Chaucer*. 10 (1988) 3–21.

———. *A Crisis of Truth: Literature and Law in Ricardian England*. Philadelphia: University of Pennsylvania Press, 1999.

————. "Palamon's Appeal of Treason in the *Knight's Tale*," in *The Letter of the Law: Legal Practice and Literary Production in Medieval England*. Ed. Emily Steiner and Candace Barrington. Ithaca, NY: Cornell University Press, 2002. pp. 105–114.

Hanawalt, Barbara. *Crime and Conflict in English Communities, 1300–1348*. Cambridge: Cambridge University Press, 1979.

————. *"Of Good and Ill Repute": Gender and Social Control in Medieval England*. Oxford: Oxford University Press, 1998.

————. "Violence in the Domestic Milieu of Late Medieval England," in *Violence in Medieval Society*. Ed. Richard Keauper. Woodbridge, Suffolk: Boydell, 2000. pp. 197–214.

Hanna, Ralph. *London Literature, 1300–1380*. Cambridge: Cambridge University Press, 2005.

Hansen, Elaine Tuttle. "'Of His Love Daungerous to Me': Liberation, Subversion, and Domestic Violence in the *Wife of Bath's Prologue* and *Tale*," in *Geoffrey Chaucer: The Wife of Bath*. Ed. Peter Beidler. Boston: Bedford, 1996. pp. 273–89.

Haskett, Timothy S. "Conscience, Justice, and Authority in the Late-Medieval English Court of Chancery," in *Expectations of the Law in the Middle Ages*. Ed. Anthony Musson. Woodbridge, Suffolk: Boydell Press, 2001. pp. 151–63.

Hasler, Anthony. "Hoccleve's Unregimented Body." *Paragraph*. 13 (1990) 164–181.

Hettinger, Madonna J. "Defining the Servant: Legal and Extra-legal Terms of Employment in Fifteenth-Century England," in *The Work of Work: Servitude, Slavery, and Labor in Medieval England*. Ed. Allen J. Frantzen and Douglad Moffat. Glasgow: Cruithne Press, 1994. pp. 206–28.

Hicks, Michael. "The 1468 Statute of Livery." *Historical Research*. 64 (1991) 15–28.

————. *Bastard Feudalism* (New York: Longman, 1995).

Hines, John, Nathalie Cohen, and Simon Roffey. "Iohannes Gower, Armiger, Poeta: Life Records and Memorials of His Life and Death," in *A Companion to Gower*. Ed. Siân Echard. Cambridge: D.S. Brewer, 2004. pp. 23–43.

Hodges, Kenneth. *Forging Communities in Malory's* Le Morte Darthur. New York: Palgrave, 2005.

Ireland, Richard. "Lucrece, Philomela (and Cecily): Chaucer and the Law of Rape," in *Crime and Punishment in the Middle Ages*. Ed. Timothy Haskett. Victoria: University of Victoria Press, 1998. pp. 37–61.

Jefferies, P.J. "Profitable Fourteenth-Century Legal Practice and Landed Investment: The Case of Judge Stonor, *c*. 1281–1354." *Southern History*. 15 (1993) 18–33.

Jewell, Helen. "*Piers Plowman*—A Poem of Crisis: An Analysis of Political Instability in Langland's England," in *Politics and Crisis in Fourteenth-Century England*. Ed. John Taylor and Wendy Childs. Gloucester: Alan Sutton, 1990. pp. 59–80.

Kaeuper, Richard. *War, Justice, and Public Order: England and France in the Later Middle Ages*. Oxford: Oxford University Press, 1988.

Kelly, Henry Ansgar. "Meanings and Uses of *Raptus* in Chaucer's Time." *Studies in the Age of Chaucer*. 20 (1998) 101–65.

Kennedy, Kathleen E. "Hoccleve's Dangerous Game of Draughts." *Notes and Queries*. N.S. 53 (2006) 410–14.

———. "Maintaining Love through Accord in the *Tale of Melibee*." *Chaucer Review*. 39 (2004) 165–76.

———. "Retaining a Court of Chancery in *Piers Plowman*." *Yearbook of Langland Studies*. 17 (2004) 175–89.

———. "Retaining Men (and a Retaining Woman) in *Piers Plowman*." *Yearbook of Langland Studies*. 20 (2007) 191–214.

Kettle, Ann J. "Ruined Maids: Prostitutes and Servant Girls in Later Medieval England," in *Matrons and Marginal Women in Medieval Society*. Ed. Robert R. Edwards and Vickie Ziegler. Woodbridge, Suffolk: Boydell Press, 1995. pp. 19–31.

Kirby, J.L. *Henry IV of England*. London: Archon Books, 1971.

Kirby, Joan. "A Fifteenth-Century Family, the Plumptons of Plumpton, and Their Lawyers, 1461–1515." *Northern History*. 25 (1989) 106–19.

Knapp, Ethan. *The Bureaucratic Muse. Thomas Hoccleve and the Literature of Late Medieval England*. University Park, PA: Pennsylvania State University Press, 2001.

Lees, Clare. "Gender and Exchange in *Piers Plowman*," in *Class and Gender in Early English Literature*. Ed. Britton J. Harwood and Gillian Overing. Bloomington, IN: Indiana University Press, 1994. pp. 112–30.

Leicester, H. Marshall. "'My Bed Was Ful of Verray Blood': Subject, Dream, and Rape in the Wife of Bath's Prologue and Tale," in *Geoffrey Chaucer: The Wife of Bath*. Ed. Peter Beidler. Boston: St. Martin's Press, 1996. pp. 235–54.

Maddern, Philippa. "'Best Trusted Friends': Concepts and Practices of Friendship among Fifteenth-century Norfolk Gentry," in *England in the Fifteenth Century: Proceedings of the 1992 Harlaxton Symposium*. Ed. Nicholas Rogers. Stamford: Paul Watkins, 1994. pp. 100–17.

———. "Honour among the Pastons: Gender and Integrity in Fifteenth-Century English Provincial Society." *Journal of Medieval History*. 14 (1988) 357–71.

———. *Violence and the Social Order: East Anglia 1422–1442*. Oxford: Clarendon Press, 1992.

Maddicott, J.R. *Law and Lordship: Royal Justices as Retainers in Thirteenth-and Fourteenth-Century England*. Oxford: Past and Present Society, 1978.

Mast, Isabelle. "Rape in John Gower's *Confessio Amantis* and Other Related Works," in *Young Medieval Women*. Ed. Katherine J. Lewis, Noël J. Menuge, and Kim Phillips. New York: St. Martin's Press, 1999. pp. 103–32.

McFarlane, K.B. *Lancastrian Kings and Lollard Knights*. Oxford: Clarendon Press, 1972.

————. *The Nobility of Later Medieval England*. Oxford: Clarendon Press, 1973.

McGregor, Francine. "What of Dorigen? Agency and Ambivalence in the *Franklin's Tale*." *Chaucer Review*. 31 (1997) 365–78.

McIntosh, Marjorie. *Working Women in English Society, 1300–1620*. Cambridge: Cambridge University Press, 2005.

Menuge, Noël James. "Female Wards and Marriage in Romance and Law: A Question of Consent," in *Young Medieval Women*. Eds. Katherine J. Lewis, Noël James Menuge, and Kim Phillips. New York: St. Martin's Press, 1999. pp. 153–71.

Middleton, Anne. "Acts of Vagrancy: The C Version 'Autobiography' and the Statute of 1388," in *Written Work: Langland, Labor, and Authorship*. Ed. Steven Justice and Kathryn Kerby-Fulton. Philadelphia: University of Pennsylvania Press, 1997. pp. 208–317.

Mortimer, Nigel. *John Lydgate's* Fall of Princes *Narrative Tragedy in its Literary and Political Contexts*. Oxford: Clarendon Press, 2005.

Musson, Anthony. *Medieval Law in Context: The Growth of Legal Consciousness from Magna Carta to the Peasants' Revolt*. Manchester: Manchester University Press, 2001.

————. *Public Order and Law Enforcement: The Local Administration of Criminal Justice 1294–1350*. Woodbridge, Suffolk: Boydell Press, 1996.

Myers, Michael. "The Failure of Conflict Resolution and the Limits of Arbitration in King's Lynn 1405–1416," in *Traditions and Transformations in Late Medieval England*. Ed. Sharon Michalove and Douglas Biggs. Boston: Brill, 2002. pp. 81–107.

Newhall, Richard Ager. *Muster and Review: A Problem of English Military Administration 1420–1440*. Cambridge: Harvard University Press, 1940.

Ormrod, Mark. "Who Was Alice Perrers?" *Chaucer Review* 40 (2006) 219–29.

Palmer, Robert C. *The County Courts of Medieval England, 1150–1350*. Princeton, NJ: Princeton University Press, 1982.

————. *English Law in the Age of the Black Death, 1348–1381*. Chapel Hill, NC: University of North Carolina Press, 1993.

Payling, Simon J. "Law and Arbitration in Nottinghamshire 1399–1461," in *People, Politics, and Community in the Later Middle Ages*. Ed. Joel Rosenthal and Colin Richmond. New York: St. Martin's Press, 1987. pp. 140–60.

Pearsall, Derek. "Hoccleve's *Regement of Princes:* The Poetics of Royal Self-Representation." *Speculum*. 69 (1994) 386–410.

Perkins, Nicholas. *Hoccleve's* Regiment of Princes: *Counsel and Constraint*. Cambridge: D.S. Brewer, 2001.

Pilbrow, Fionn, "The Knights of the Bath: Dubbing to Knighthood in Lancastrian and Yorkist England," in *Heraldry, Pageantry and Social Display in Medieval England*. Ed. Peter Coss and Maurice Keen. Woodbridge, Suffolk: Boydell Press, 2002. pp. 195–218.

Porter, Elizabeth. "Gower's Ethical Microcosm and Political Macrocosm," in *Gower's* Confessio Amantis: *Responses and Reassessments*. Ed. A.J. Minnis. Cambridge: D.S. Brewer, 1983. pp. 135–62.

Powell, Edward. "Arbitration and the Law in England in the Late Middle Ages." *Transactions of the Royal Historical Society*. 5th ser. 33 (1983) 49–67.

———. *Kingship, Law, and Society: Criminal Justice in the Reign of Henry V.* Oxford: Clarendon Press, 1989.

Radulescu, Raluca. *The Gentry Context for Malory's* Morte Darthur. Woodbridge, Suffolk: D.S. Brewer, 2003.

Ramsey, N.L. "What Was the Legal Profession?" in *Profit, Piety, and the Professions in Later Medieval England*. Ed. Michael Hicks. Gloucester: Alan Sutton, 1990. pp. 62–71.

Rawcliffe, Carole. "The Great Lord as Peacekeeper: Arbitration by English Noblemen and Their Councils in the Later Middle Ages," in *Law and Social Change in British History*. Ed. J.A. Guy and H.G. Beale. London: Royal Historical Society, 1984. pp. 34–54.

———. "Parliament and the Settlement of Disputes by Arbitration in the late Middle Ages." *Parliamentary History*. 9 (1990) 316–342.

———. " 'That Kindliness Should be Cherished More, and Discord Driven Out': The Settlement of Commercial Disputes by Arbitration in Later Medieval England," in *Enterprise and Individuals in Fifteenth-Century England*. Ed. Jennifer Kermode. Alan Sutton: Stroud, Gloucestershire, 1991. pp. 99–117.

Rawcliffe, Carole, and Susan Flower. "English Noblemen and Their Advisers: Consultation and Collaboration in the Later Middle Ages." *Journal of British Studies*. 25 (1986) 157–77.

Raybin, David. " 'Wommen, of Kynde, Desiren Libertee': Rereading Dorigen, Rereading Marriage." *Chaucer Review*. 27 (1992) 65–86.

Richman, Gerald. "Rape and Desire in *The Wife of Bath's Tale*." *Studia Neophilologica*. 61 (1989) 161–65.

Richmond, Colin. "Elizabeth Clere: Friend of the Pastons," in *Medieval Women: Texts and Contexts in Late Medieval Britain: Essays for Felicity Riddy*. Ed. Jocelyn Wogan-Browne, Rosalyn Voaden, Arlyn Diamond, Ann Hutchison, Carol Meale, and Lesley Johnson. Turnhout, Belgium: Brepols, 2000. pp. 251–73.

———. *The Paston Family in the Fifteenth Century: The First Phase*. Cambridge: Cambridge University Press, 1990.

Robertson, Elizabeth. "Marriage, Mutual Consent, and the Affirmation of the Female Subject in the *Knight's Tale*, the *Wife of Bath's Tale*, and the *Franklin's Tale*," in *Drama, Narrative, and Poetry in the Canterbury Tales*. Ed. Wendy Harding. Toulouse: Publications Universitaire de Mirail, 2003. pp. 175–93.

———. "Public Bodies and Psychic Domains: Rape, Consent, and Female Subjectivity in Geoffrey Chaucer's *Troilus and Criseyde*," in *Representing Rape in Medieval and Early Modern Literature*. Ed. Elizabeth Robertson and Christine Rose. New York: Palgrave, 2001. pp. 282–310.

———. " 'Raptus' and the Poetics of Married Love in Chaucer's Wife of Bath's Tale and James I's *Kingis Quair*," in *Reading Medieval Culture: Essays in Honor of Robert W. Hanning*. Ed. Robert M. Stein and Sandra Pierson Prior. Notre Dame, IN: University of Notre Dame Press, 2005. pp. 302–23.

Rose, Christine. "Reading Chaucer Reading Rape," in *Representing Rape in Medieval and Early Modern Literature*. Ed. Elizabeth Robertson and Christine Rose. New York: Palgrave, 2001. pp. 21–60.

Rossi-Reder, Andrea. "Male Movement and Female Fixity in the *Franklin's Tale* and *Il Filocolo*," in *Masculinities in Chaucer: Approaches to Maleness in the* Canterbury Tales *and* Troilus and Criseyde. Ed. Peter Beidler. Cambridge: D.S. Brewer, 1998. pp. 105–16.

Rowney, Ian. "Arbitration in Gentry Disputes of the Later Middle Ages." *History*. 67 (1982) 367–74.

Saul, Nigel. *Richard II*. New Haven, CT: Yale University Press, 1997.

———. "The Commons and the Abolition of Badges." *Parliamentary History* 9 (1990) 302–15.

Saunders, Corinne. *Rape and Ravishment in the Literature of the Middle Ages*. Cambridge: D.S. Brewer, 2001.

Scanlon, Larry. *Narrative, Authority, and Power. The Medieval Exemplum and the Chaucerian Tradition*. Cambridge: Cambridge University Press, 1994.

Seabourne, Gwen. "Law, Morals and Money: Royal Regulation of the Substance of Subjects' Sales and Loans in England, 1272–1399," in *Expectations of the Law in the Middle Ages*. Ed. Anthony Musson. Woodbridge, Suffolk: Boydell Press, 2001. pp. 117–79.

Shaw, David Gary. *Necessary Conjunctions: The Social Self in Medieval England*. New York: Palgrave, 2005.

Shenk, Robert. "The Liberation of the 'Loathly Lady' of Medieval Romance." *Journal of the Rocky Mountain Medieval and Renaissance Association*. 2 (1981) 69–77.

Simpson, James. "Nobody's Man: Thomas Hoccleve's *Regiment of Princes*," in *London and Europe in the Later Middle Ages*. Ed. Julia Boffey and Pamela King. London: University of London, 1995. pp. 149–80.

Smith, David. "Disputes and Settlements in Medieval Wales: The Role of Arbitration." *The English Historical Review*. 106 (1991) 835–860.

Squibb, G.D. *The High Court of Chivalry*. Oxford: Clarendon Press, 1959.

Staley, Lynn. "Inverse Counsel: Contexts for the *Melibee*." *Studies in Philology*. 87 (1990) 137–55.

Stokes, Myra. *Justice and Mercy in* Piers Plowman. *A Reading of the B Text Visio*. London: Croom Helm, 1984.

Storey, R.L. "Liveries and Commissions of the Peace 1388–90," in *The Reign of Richard II. Essays in Honour of May McKisack*. Ed. F.R.H. Du Boulay and Caroline M. Barron. London: University of London Press, 1971. pp. 131–52.

Strohm, Paul. *England's Empty Throne. Usurpation and the Language of Legitimation, 1399–1422*. London: Yale University Press, 1998.

———. *Politique: Languages of Statecraft between Chaucer and Shakespeare*. Notre Dame, IN: University of Notre Dame Press, 2005.

Sylvester, Louise. "Reading Narratives of Rape: The Story of Lucretia in Chaucer, Gower, and Christine de Pizan." *Leeds Studies in English*. 31 (2000) 115–44.

Taylor, Mark N. "Servant and Lord/ Lady and Wife: The *Franklin's tale* and Traditions of Courtly and Conjugal Love." *Chaucer Review*. 32 (1997) 64–81.

Tilsey, David. "Arbitration in Gentry Disputes: The Case of Bucklow Hundred in Cheshire, 1400–1465," in *Courts, Counties, and the Capital in the Later Middle Ages*. Ed. Diana E.S. Dunn. New York: St. Martin's Press, 1996. pp. 53–70.

Toulmie, Sarah. "The *Prive Scilence* of Thomas Hoccleve." *Studies in the Age of Chaucer*. 22 (2000) 281–309.

Tout, T.F. *Chapters in the Administrative History of Mediæval England*. Manchester: Manchester University Press, 1930.

Trigg, Stephanie. "The Traffic in Medieval Women: Alice Perrers, Feminist Criticism and *Piers Plowman*." *Yearbook of Langland Studies*. 12 (1998) 5–29.

Tubbs, J.W. *The Common Law Mind: Medieval and Early Modern Conceptions*. Baltimore: Johns Hopkins University Press, 2000.

Tucker, P. "The Early History of the Court of Chancery: A Comparative Study." *English Historical Review.* 115 (2000) 791–811.

Van Dyke, Carolynn. *Chaucer's Agents: Cause and Representation in Chaucerian Narrative.* Cranbury, NJ: Fairleigh Dickinson University Press, 2005.

———. "The Clerk's and the Franklin's Subjected Subjects." *Studies in the Age of Chaucer.* 17 (1995) 45–68.

Walker, Simon. *The Lancastrian Affinity, 1361–1399.* Oxford: Clarendon Press, 1990.

Walker, Sue Sheridan. "The Feudal Family and the Common Law Courts: The Pleas Protecting Rights of Wardship and Marriage, c. 1225–1375." *Journal of Medieval History.* 14 (1988) 13–31.

———. "Punishing Convicted Ravishers: Statutory Strictures and Actual Practice in Thirteenth and Fourteenth-Century England." *Journal of Medieval History.* 13 (1987) 237–50.

Wallace, David. *Chaucerian Polity: Absolutist Lineages and Associational Forms in England and Italy.* Stanford, CA: Stanford University Press, 1997.

Walling, Amanda, "'In Hir Tellyng Difference': Gender, Authority, and Interpretation in the *Tale of Melibee*." *Chaucer Review* 40 (2005) 163–81.

Warner, Lawrence. "The Ur-B of *Piers Plowman* and the Earliest Production of C and B." *Yearbook of Langland Studies.* 16 (2002) 3–39.

Watts, John. "Looking for the State in Medieval England," in *Heraldry, Pageantry and Social Display in Medieval England.* Ed. Peter Coss and Maurice Keen. Woodbridge, Suffolk: Boydell Press, 2002. pp. 243–67.

Wilcock, Ruth. "Local Disorder in the Honour of Knaresborough, c. 1438–1461 and the National Context." *Northern History.* 41 (2004) 39–80.

Yeager, Robert. "John Gower's French," in *A Companion to Gower.* Ed. Sîan Echard. Woodbridge, Suffolk: Boydell, 2004. pp. 137–52.

INDEX

abbot-monk relationships,
    121n5, 122n5
    See also unequal relationships
accords, 62–3, 64–5, 72, 138n13
affines. *See* knights; retainers
affinities, 7, 78
    royal, 62, 76, 80–2, 145n85
    See also Lancastrian affinities
agency
    vs. autonomy, 38, 52, 123n11
    and common law, 66–7
    male *vs.* female, 36, 132n45
    of raped women, 42, 43, 52
    royal, 102–3
    suicide and, 44
    See also autonomy; sliding agency
allegory, 68, 73, 76
Alliterative Morte Darthur, 81
annuities, 7–8, 109, 153n44
    See also remuneration
Anstis, John, 83
aporia, 42, 44–5
Appellant crisis of 1388, 104
appointements, 21–2, 126n29
Articles of Deposition (1399), 77,
    145nn78, 82
Assize of Bread and Beer (1257), 98,
    152n37
Assize of Weights and Measures
    (1303), 152n37
attorneys. *See* lawyers; legal
    professionals
autonomy
    vs. agency, 38, 52, 123n11
    of husbands, 37, 44–5, 54, 56–7, 59

of judges, 92–3
of legal professionals, 13, 89,
    92–3, 94
modern *vs.* medieval ideas of,
    5–6, 119
oaths and, 56, 58
of retainers, 40, 55, 57–9, 66,
    74, 75
of wives, 34–6, 37–9, 40–1, 45,
    53–4, 66, 67–8
    See also agency; sliding agency

badges. *See* livery
bailiffs, 69, 91, 96–7
    See also legal professionals
Baker, J.H., 99–100, 122n6,
    151nn20,31
Baldwin, Anna, 141n33, 143n59
Barr, Helen, 145n78
Bean, J.M.W., 7–8
Beaufort family, 16
Belknap, Sir Robert, 122n6, 142n40
Bellamy, J.G., 9–10, 11
Bergen, Henry, 81
Bertholet, Craig, 42
Biggs, Douglas, 100, 142n42
Black Death, 152n37
Black Panthers, 121n1
Blanch, Robert, 55
Bolingbroke, Henry, Earl of Derby.
    See Henry IV
Brand, Paul, 98–9
bribery. *See* corruption; embracery
Brown, Carole Koepke, 136n116
bureaucratic work, 108–9, 114